# MONEY

## The New Science of Making It

Scott F. Paradis

http://Success101Workshop.com

# Books by
# Scott F. Paradis:

*Money*
*The New Science of Making It*

*High Performance Health and Fitness Habits*
*Engage Your Health and Fitness Auto-Pilot*

*High Performance Habits*
*Making Success a Habit*

*How to Succeed at Anything*
*In 3 Simple Steps*

*Success 101 How Life Works*
*Know the Rules, Play to Win*

*Warriors Diplomats Heroes*
*Why America's Army Succeeds*
*Lessons for Business and Life*

*Promise and Potential*
*A Life of Wisdom, Courage, Strength, and Will*

**And coming soon:**

*Build Me a Son*
*A story of Hope and Courage*

*Be*
*A Messenger of Hope,*
*An Example of Faith and an Expression of Love*

*Are You Really Better Than Average?*
*Where You Stand and the Fastest Way to the Top*

Change your life with these online courses and workshops by
# Scott F. Paradis:

*Money*
*The New Science of Making It*
*www.Success101Money.com*

*High Performance Health and Fitness Habits*
*Engage Your Health and Fitness Auto-Pilot*
*www.Success101Health.com*

*High Performance Habits*
*Making Success a Habit*
*www.Success101Habits.com*

*Success 101 How to Succeed*
*Focus on Fundamentals*
*www.Success101Succeed.com*

*Success 101 How Life Works*
*Know the Rules, Play to Win*

*High Performance Leadership*
*Fundamental Leadership Habits*

*Loving 101*
*Making Love a Habit*

*Be*
*A Messenger of Hope,*
*An Example of Faith and an Expression of Love*

# *MONEY*
## *The New Science of Making It*

Copyright © 2015 Scott F. Paradis

The information presented herein represents the views of the author. These views may change. While every attempt has been made to verify the information in this book, the author does not assume any responsibility for errors, inaccuracies, or omissions.

Published and distributed by:

Cornerstone Achievements
New Hampshire and Virginia, USA
*www.cornerstone-achievements.com*

ISBN (ebook): 978-0-9863821-2-3
ISBN (paperback): 978-0-9863821-3-0

Published in the United States of America.

This book is dedicated to every person creating and contributing value to this world.

Your contribution adds zest to life, keep making it.

# TABLE OF CONTENTS

# PART 4: Alchemy, All that Glitters Isn't Gold

# PREFACE

The best business schools in America, Wharton, Harvard and Stanford among them teach prospective industry leaders about the economics of supply and demand, about finance and financial accounting, and about management, marketing and operations. With enthusiasm and academic rigor business schools teach how to optimize production and distribution with an intent to maximize profit and crush the competition. It is after all a "dog eat dog world." It's nothing personal, it's just business. The problem is the premise is wrong. It's not just business, it's always personal.

Making money is an intensely personal endeavor. *Money, The New Science of Making It* attempts to bridge the gap between the business dogma so many look to implement and the fundamental truths behind money and markets. Keep an open mind. If you do, you will find something unexpected and something delightful. You will come to look at making money from an entirely new perspective; and that might be just the change you need.

## Two Notes Regarding Style

First, by design you will find *Money, The New Science of Making It* repetitious. We expand our thinking and build new habits by repetition. I have attempted to walk a fine line emphasizing key points "just enough" to sink in, rather than "too much" to annoy. Please forgive me if I cross the line. Second, you probably have noticed my writing does not conform to AP style. My approach is informal, you might say conversational. Some sentences begin with *ands* and *buts* and end with prepositions. My intent is to communicate with you as effectively and directly as possible. Please forgive any lack of elegance and don't get bogged down with words; sift for meaning. Connect with the truths the words are meant to convey.

## What if...

Do you ever wonder, what if? "What if instead of procrastinating I embrace the opportunity? What if instead of rationalizing and making excuses I just move forward? And what if instead of judging and condemning and blaming, myself and others, I just accept what is and set about creating something better?" Well, it's time to stop wondering what if. It's time to make a change. Understand and apply the fundamentals and make money.

# FOREWORD

# MAKE IT OR TAKE IT

Every fork in the road is a decision point. The question you must ask yourself, "Do I go right or left or do nothing at all?" Every choice comes with a built-in opportunity cost; something we give up, something we miss out on in choosing one way over another. Doing nothing is not an option. Oh, sure it's an option, a selection; we can sit idly by and wait. One thing is for sure, even when choosing a "wait and see" strategy circumstances will change; that is the nature of life. But the opportunity costs for a wait and see strategy can be exorbitant. Time waits for no one; and time is the one asset we have in limited supply. You picked up this book not to waste time, but with the hope of propelling yourself into a new reality, an abundant, prosperous reality of making it. Choose to move forward, choose to do something.

Before we begin in earnest we reach our first fork in the road.

You and I both know few things in life are black and white, most decision points present in many shades of gray. Here however, I offer a stark contrast between two alternatives. This is an artificial distinction, but it is one we do well to draw. When it comes to amassing wealth; to acquiring money and all money represents, we must choose between two well-defined alternative paths. One leads to growth and fulfillment, abundance and prosperity; the other to competition and conflict, scarcity and lack. To amass wealth, to acquire money we can choose either to "make it" or "take it". There is more than enough for everyone, but each path, "make it" or "take it" leads to very different results.

This book, **Money, The New Science of Making It**, focuses on the "make it" choice.

Money isn't everything, but money certainly is a magical component of our existence in this modern, material world. We don't need money to survive and thrive but we absolutely need what money represents. Money represents freedom and flexibility, autonomy and a sense of security. Having money allows an individual a multitude of options. And while everyone has the opportunity to make money, far too many people decide to take what they want.

Making money is a creative, cooperative, life-enhancing activity. We create when we let the energy of life flow through us into this world. We make money by giving of ourselves, our time, energy and talent; by contributing to and serving others. We make money by helping people get what they want. We make money; we experience the energy of an abundant flow, when we cooperate with life; when we help life expand.

Time and opportunity are two constants of our temporary existence. As long as we live we have time and opportunity. Every second life presents opportunities; opportunities to explore and experience, opportunities to learn and grow; and opportunities to create and contribute. Life never stops presenting opportunities but the clock never stops either. Time keeps ticking away. We are left to choose. We must choose what to do with each opportunity. We can choose to make the most of an opportunity or let it pass by. Choosing to make money is a choice to create and contribute; a choice to add value to life. Choosing to create and contribute is never the wrong choice.

4

Taking money on the other hand is a disruptive, ultimately life-draining activity. We take money when we compete to beat someone, not to get better ourselves. We take money by deceiving and stealing, intimidating and extorting. We take when we seek to harvest what we have not sown. We take when we forcibly divert other people's creations to self-serving purposes. Taking money appears to be lucrative, and in the short term it may be, but ultimately taking money limits the takers growth and undermines the entire economic system.

Life doesn't happen to you so much as life happens through you. Money, wealth and riches, are a manifestation of the energy of life. How one goes about acquiring wealth and riches; how one goes about getting money matters.

*Money, The New Science of Making It* is a scientific exploration. We examine and asses a specific money making process. That process is about doing things a certain way; a scientific way. When you do things a certain way you produce exactly the results you desire, the right results and the best results: wealth and prosperity for you and your family.

If you are not prosperous and wealthy today, it's not because you lack something. You have everything you need to succeed and succeed spectacularly. You have all you need to make lots of money. You don't "need" something different. You must first "be" different and then supported from a solid foundation, do something different.

In this life you get what you give. Give more; get more. Don't take money. Make money. Create and contribute. This is the path to a bright future; the path for a peaceful and prosperous world.

Do the right things; those few simple things to generate wealth; to create and contribute. You are meant to live a full and fulfilling life. You are meant to experience the good things here and now. Apply the science and make it.

*Money, The New Science of Making It* is divided into four parts. *Part 1* explores and defines just what money is. *Part 2* lays out the tools of the trade and the characteristics of the collective system. *Part 3* translates the "system" into something anyone can work with to make money. And *Part 4* explains the science, the process producing precise results.

People have always valued gold and silver. Precious metals have been used to adorn bodies as jewelry, embellish cherished objects and decorate important structures. Gold and silver have been, for thousands of years, the most widely used form of money on the planet. Gold was still an essential part of the global monetary system up until 1971. Even though gold has been replaced by government guarantees (in the form of dollars, Euro, Yen, Yuan, etc.) gold is still a highly valued commodity. People to this day, pan for riches, sifting through sand and silt to find a golden treasure.

Each chapter and the Foreword of *Money* closes with a summary section titled: *Panning for Gold*. Each *Panning for Gold* section is a collection of insightful nuggets from that chapter. The final chapter, *Prospectors, Miners and Merchants Panning for Gold* (Chapter 17), is a compilation of all the golden nuggets from *Money, The New Science of Making It*.

You can have more, do more and be more. You can be wealthy. You can make money. There is a science to it. You must do something. Employ the science.

6

## Panning for Gold:

- People can make money or take money.

- Making money is a creative, value-generating and life-enhancing process.

- Making money is being a conduit for energy to flow into and through the world.

- Taking money is a coercive, destructive and ultimately life-draining process.

- Taking money is siphoning off energy from an existing flow.

- The choice is always yours. Choose to make it, not take it.

# PART 1

## MONEY MAKES

## THE WORLD GO ROUND

People think of money as something discrete, tangible and valuable. Money is that "thing" we all want more of. People invest more time, energy and effort into getting money than virtually any other aspect of their adult lives. Most people however, are mistaken about what money is and what money represents. Money, money, money; the currency of trust; is always a means to an end.

# CHAPTER 1

# FAMILY MONEY

## Unity, Integrity, Industry

### Who You Know and What You Know

Britain's *Daily Telegraph* decreed, "This multinational banking family is a byword for wealth, power and discretion…The Rothschild name has become synonymous with money and power to a degree that perhaps no other family has ever matched." Kings and queens, princes and popes, governments and principalities did not act but with consent of the Rothschild's.

How did one man starting from a crowded tenement house in a Frankfurt ghetto establish the wealthiest and most powerful family in the world?

By building relationships, leveraging trust, and employing a new social technology to exploit man's unbridled lust for power. And by enabling the energy of ambition being unleashed around the world through an industrial revolution. The Rothschild's facilitated the flow of money for audacious opportunities and tragic follies alike. However things turned out for their clients, the Rothschild family managed their commitments such that the one thing they assured was fortune for themselves; as fortune favors the bold.

The Rothschild's business was money. They traded in money. They leveraged the power money represented so astutely they were able to rise from virtual obscurity to the crest of international finance and political influence in two generations. That vast fortune built in international finance two hundred years ago exists today as the Rothschild's may still be the wealthiest family in the history of the world.

The Rothschild family's move from merchant and money-changing pursuits to international banking and finance began with Mayer Amschel Rothschild. Mayer, initially destined to be a rabbi, as a boy while helping with his father's small banking business developed an interest in coins. After some religious study, Mayer determined to change his career from decidedly otherworldly, to a most conspicuously worldly focus. He apprenticed at an Oppenheim banking-house in Hanover. After his father's passing Mayer returned to Frankfurt and opened a business of his own. He served as a general agent and banker, and traded in art, coins and other collectibles.

While Mayer did not have the advantage of social status, as Jews were a disadvantaged minority in Europe, he did benefit from some shrewd and farsighted choices. He chose as his vocation money; something in high demand, particularly among the elite. He leveraged relationships, most notably with a nearby prince who happened to control the largest private fortune in Europe. And he married well. He and his wife Guttle together had five sons and five daughters. Those sons became the cornerstones upon which the family dynasty rested. Guttle lived to see her sons become the most influential men in all of Europe and arguably the world.

Mayer's father had traded with Prince William of Hesse and had built a reputation for integrity. With some bold maneuvering and tenacity Mayer was able to secure Prince William as a customer of his. Upon the death of the Prince's father William inherited the largest private fortune in Europe. Mayer was appointed an agent of the court. He served as a banker for the royals and brokered international financial agreements.

Mayer Rothschild's business prospered. He built relationships within the tight-knit, mostly Jewish community of bankers and financiers, and he retained as customers and clients the wealthiest nobility in his region. But Mayer had a vision that saw opportunity well beyond the Rhine River valley. As the nineteenth century dawned Mayer began to dispatch his sons to the seats of financial power around the continent. By 1812 (the year Mayer died) he had banking and finance operations in Frankfurt, Vienna, Naples, London and Paris each run by one of his sons.

The Rothschild's leveraged their relationships with royalty and quietly but deliberately expanded operations. Mayer and his sons recognized information was the master-key to riches in the finance game. The brothers built an efficient system of couriers, and what their competition called "spies" around the continent, so they could routinely communicate with one another; sharing key business, financial and political information. The Rothschild's gathered and disseminated critical information faster than any of their competition. This cost the Rothschild's competition dearly.

## Taking Risks

Through disciplined lending and investing the Rothschild's became a financial force to be reckoned with on the continent. It was however, the ambition of one despot which provided the opportunity for spectacular gain. Squabbling amongst nobles seemed to be the most popular pastime in Europe. In the feudal, city-state system still dominating Europe most monarchies operated by means of tribute; conquering and plundering were the way to get ahead. Though times were changing, the ambition of one man, Napoleon Bonaparte, became legendary. Napoleon, the ever-ambitious ruler of France, sought to make himself emperor of Europe.

War was the opportunity the Rothschild's organized to take advantage of. The prosecution of a war requires money on a scale necessitating international finance. The on-again, off-again wars on the European continent were each an opportunity for profit, but the "big one" came with the culmination of the struggle against Napoleon at Waterloo.

Nathan Rothschild, the family principle in London, brokered a deal to finance the Duke of Wellington fighting against Napoleon. Through their network the Rothschild's were able to surreptitiously supply the Duke of Wellington all the gold specie he needed to effectively conduct his campaign on the continent. The Rothschild's primary means of financing war debt was through the issuance of bonds. Choosing the wrong side to back in a war could be a risky proposition for financiers, but the Rothschild's innovated to ensure they minimized risk.

The Rothschild's were so well connected they often financed both sides of a conflict. In the case of the show-down at Waterloo however, Nathan's tactical maneuvering proved to be the most profitable of all. First, Nathan was active at the London stock exchange. Because of his network of informants Nathan Rothschild new the outcome of the Battle of Waterloo well before anyone else on the trading floor. On the first trading day after the battle, but before most people knew the outcome, Nathan began selling. Other traders, knowing the Rothschild's were well-informed and seeing Nathan sell followed his lead. Soon the market was in a panic. Rothschild waited until the brokers were in a frenzy and then he had his agents begin to buy, at pennies on the dollar. When word of the outcome of Waterloo did reach

Rothschild's competitors they realized they had been duped. Rothschild walked away with sizable trading profits that day.

A few hours work on the trading floor however, was not the grand opportunity for Rothschild. He saw a larger prize in the offing. To finance the war Rothschild had issued long-term bonds. Typically with "war financing" prices of bonds would rise and fall along with the tide of battle. When a war concluded funds were no longer required and the bonds would usually decline in value until they were liquidated. Because the war between the England and the other European powers against France was over so quickly it seemed the opportunity for profit would too be lost. But Rothschild made a shrewd calculation. He wagered heavily that with reparations and accelerating industrial development requiring money, British bonds would in fact appreciate. His gamble paid off handsomely. This one move in the bond market brought the Rothschild's a vast fortune. With those profits they were able to secure their empire by financing the industrialization of Europe and bold projects to enhance trade and globalization around the world.

## From Ambitious to Audacious

"Unity, Integrity, Industry" was the Rothschild family motto. Mayer Rothschild structured the family business, and even specified in his will, that the family was to remain tight-knit and guarded. Their books were never to be opened to an inquisitive world. The relationships they formed and nurtured were essential to their success. They had to remain united to achieve the audacious goals they set for themselves.

The business of money is the business of trust. To build any type of financial organization and to endure a financier must do what he says and deliver what he promises. Long-term success with customer and clients' money

15

requires minimizing risk. Integrity is the watchword in an industry of trust.

The Rothschild's were nothing if not industrious. They learned what they needed to learn; they forged relationships and built networks to advance their cause. They innovated when they needed to innovate; they took risks when they thought it was right and prudent to take risks. The Rothschild's held true to their motto, "Unity, Integrity, Industry" as they saw it. They commanded the high-ground in an industry in its infancy, international finance, and they amassed a fortune perhaps unparalleled in the history of mankind.

The ascent of money made for a new world order.

## Panning for Gold

- Focus on existing opportunities or create new opportunities.
- Acquire "valuable" knowledge.
- Build, nurture and sustain relationships with people you trust.
- Take calculated risks.
- Do what you say you will do, and deliver value.

# CHAPTER 2

# MONEY, MONEY, MONEY

## Something more than money makes the world go round.

## What is money? The Traditional View

The American Heritage Dictionary defines money as: "A medium that can be exchanged for goods and services and is used as a measure of their values on the market, including among its forms a commodity such as gold, an officially issued coin or note, or a deposit in a checking account or other readily liquefiable account." Wikipedia goes on: "In common usage, money refers more specifically to currency, particularly the many circulating currencies with legal tender status conferred by a nation state; recently deposit accounts denominated in such currencies have come to be considered part of the money supply."

The formal, traditional, concise definition of money:

Money is:

    1. A medium of exchange

    2. A unit of account

    3. A store of value.

Money serves as our means of getting what we want, a medium of exchange, in the nearly inexhaustible market of goods and services. Money serves as a measure of accounting for value. We can and do keep score, keep account of our belongings, and our status relative to other people, by converting and measuring our assets in the common expressions, unit of measure or unit of account, of money. And money serves as a standard, universal and impersonal store of value. We confer to money properties equating to tangible things: products; the energy of labor applied to tasks: services; and information and ideas. The conventional mainstream view holds that money, whether in the form of a coin, a note, a commodity or a promise is a thing of real and enduring value. But is that what money really is?

## The Advance of Money

Most human beings, most of us, are realists. Not "realists" in terms of being pragmatic and practical, although we may be; most of us are realists in that we deal with things, life in its tangible, touchable, malleable form. We are realists in that, for the most part, we are only definitely persuaded if we can see it, touch it, taste it, smell it, and or hear it; if we can experience or feel it through our bodies. We are most pragmatic and practical with stuff: things we don't have to argue about or convince others or ourselves, are real. When it comes to money, most of us are in the same boat: we are committed to the view that money is something real and tangible; something we can see and touch and taste and hear and smell. Is it?

We put our trust in money. Is money what we really trust?

The age-old view is that money grew out of a system of barter. Barter was a trade between two people with two distinct offers (products or services). Each party to a trade had to be willing to accept what the other party offered in this simple two-way exchange. If one party to a barter transaction didn't have exactly what the other wanted he would have to look for a second, third, fourth or perhaps a fifth party to trade with until he got what he was after.

To improve on barter and facilitate the exchange of goods and services people settled on a relatively "liquid" medium; what we call money.  Different groups settled on different mediums.  Amongst different people at different times and locations these "mediums" ranged from cattle, to seashells, to stones, to salt, to chocolate, to precious metals, to paper notes and so on.  Conferring value to a medium of exchange and then conducting transactions in that medium permitted a more open, expedient and convenient market.  Money streamlined the process of trade, saving time, energy and effort.

A remarkable outcome of this social advance, money, was the specialization of labor it allowed.  No longer did a small group, a family or clan, have to be "jacks of all trade".  No longer did a family or tribe have to find, acquire or produce everything it needed.  With a system of money, an individual or a group of people could more eagerly and easily focus on what they could do best and what they liked to do most, and or they could focus on exploiting whatever resources were most readily available.  That specialization of labor in turn promoted more populous settlements and greater urbanization.

As money evolved it advantaged individuals and groups economically while challenging political tradition.  As the influence of money grew; as money was ascribed with more value; society became less constrained by the tribute model of hereditary hierarchy and social caste.  A system of money allowed individuals to improve their position in society and it allowed society to organize more efficiently and produce more effectively.

The specialization of labor and the emancipation of political power allowed for great strides forward in cultural organization and human productivity. The advantages a money system provided drove a, some might say "virtuous" cycle of progress in cultural affairs. But money, like every other artifact of human engineering also had a downside. Money in modern society came to serve as the master key unlocking all types of pleasures and quite frequently it came to serve as a force unleashing all sorts of pain.

Using an agreed upon medium to serve as a temporary store of value, people looking to avail themselves of a wide range of products and services or to pay tribute or taxes for that matter, did not have to produce a specific commodity to exchange. All they needed was money; that medium, whatever it was. People had to provide something of value to others to get money, but money itself was ascribed with value; an impersonal but agreed upon value.

Money was itself a medium of exchange storing value. Money made economic exchanges, the market, trade, impersonal. And money became equated with what money could buy. Money offered society increased productivity and a host of other benefits; first among these, an increasing supply of goods and services to satisfy an endless array of wants and needs. Money freed up political power and unshackled endless ambition and insatiable desires. But this still isn't the whole story. This isn't the true miracle of money.

## An Even More Sophisticated System

Barter is a system of bilateral exchange: a transfer of goods and or services between two willing parties. Another element however, was involved in the developing nature of trade, of markets, and the evolution of the system of money; that other element was time.

Let's look at a simplified theoretical example of a hunter trading with a farmer.

A hunter and a farmer have a relationship. The hunter kills a deer and desires to trade with the farmer. Venison is a perishable commodity, but the crops the hunter wants are not ready for harvest yet. The hunter gives the farmer venison now and secures a promise from the farmer for crops to be provided in the future. To compensate for the delay in time the farmer will deliver more crops than he would have if he had conducted a timely barter exchange. The hunter provides a product now and in return gets a credit (the credit of those crops; with an agreed upon premium added to make up for time) for use in the future. The farmer receives meat and incurs a debt. The hunter holds a current credit and the farmer owes a debt against a future harvest.

The circumstances of this exchange could easily be reversed. Say it was harvest time and the farmer provides grain to the hunter now, a credit, against the promise, a debit or debt, for venison in the future. Credits and debits, an enhanced means of exchange, is a system incorporating and allowing for the natural functioning of time. The value of time factors into this system of exchange. While people expect real "things" to change hands, promises, "trust" really drives the system.

Advancing still farther: What if the hunter, or the farmer in the second case, does not want to wait for some time in the future? Can he transfer his credit? Can this credit, something the holder has value, be transferred to a third party?

The credit and debit practice is, like barter, a process of bilateral exchange. A credit and debit system has advantages; however it is constrained much like barter. A barter system or a system of credits and debits (mutual assurances based on personal trust) are constrained by relationships; the personal relationship and trust one has with another; and the specific types of goods and services involved in the exchange.  This limits liquidity.  The value of the exchange is constrained by the relationship.  The trust, the basis for credits and debits, is a factor of a bond, one person to another.  What if the bond were loosened?

People recognized the limits inherent in barter and the time-dependent system of credits and debits.  People took advantage of opportunity.  Incorporating the time elements of credits and debits, people invented a social technology to revolutionize the world.  They created a social system beyond the typical view of money as: a medium of exchange, a unit of account, and a store of value: a tangible thing.  They conceived of and employed a social system, the centerpiece of which was money, to leverage people's energy and efforts and build an even more dynamic and expansive system of trade.

In an impersonal society, which a monetary system facilitates, people prefer to trust in tangible things rather than intangible things.   However today we trust, almost absolutely, the value the medium represents (dollars, Euros, Yen, Yuan in currency or on account) over the physical properties of that currency (paper or electronic digits).  We confer to the medium the value of what the medium can obtain.

Looking more closely we realize something else is the basis for money.  Money is not really a thing at all.  Money is a social technology, a sophisticated social technology we employ to order our world.

We usually and typically equate money with currency; that tangible, "value-laden" commodity; when in fact money is not a physical commodity at all.  A more comprehensive definition of money (but still not complete for unlocking the miracle of money) views this social technology of "the money system" as more than trade facilitated by the exchange of a commodity. Rather money is a social technology; a social technology facilitating economic activity. A more comprehensive view of money delineates a system composed of three fundamental elements:

1. An abstract unit of value denominating a currency (abstract unit = unit of account; currency = medium of exchange; value = store of value; we convert value into a mathematical standard)

2. A system of tracking credit and debit balances (record keeping)

3. The possibility of transferring a credit (the debtor's obligation) without limitation

The real value of money is the system; not the commodity. Money facilitates trade which in turn drives what people do best: create and consume. Money facilitates people producing and consuming more.

But even this is not the whole picture. The miracle of money rests in something entirely human and something much more profound. Something we will explore next.

## Panning for Gold

- The traditional definition of money (medium of exchange, unit of account, store of value) does not go far enough.
- Money streamlines the process of trade, saving time, energy and effort.
- Money promotes the specialization of labor.
- As more people trusted in the medium, money became synonymous with the things money could buy.
- Not everything money offers is an advance.
- Money alters the political and social landscape.
- Money is impersonal.
- Money frees up political power and unshackles ambition and desire.
- A monetary system incorporates the element of time in a system of trading and tracking credits and debits.
- Money is a sophisticated social technology we employ to order our world.

# CHAPTER 3

# THE CURRENCY OF TRUST

**Money may not buy happiness but it sure makes being miserable more tolerable.**

## It's about Relationships and Feelings

The genius of money is not a as means to facilitate economic transactions. The genius of money is the social system it empowers. It's not the only social system, but it is far-and-away the most pervasive system driving human action today on this planet; more so for some, less so for others.

The advent of a money system allowed a break with tradition; a break with the social order of the past. A money system divorces value from specific people and things. Money lets individuals and groups make their own way in society. Individuals and groups can live, move, and progress, not based on tradition or heredity or caste but based on the ability to generate or acquire something of value; the universal measure of which is money. This social system, the system with money at the center however, is far from utopian.

Economists, academics, and financial gurus all seek to demystify and exploit the workings of supposedly rational free markets: our "system of money". In their haste to uncover enduring wisdom or secure a path to fame and fortune, learned theorists often overlook the most fundamental and significant aspect of money and markets: people.

If we were to attempt to assess the worth of all items with economic value in this world, from tangible, physical things to ideas, we undoubtedly would ascribe a sum in the hundreds of trillions of dollars. This is what we do within a money system: measure everything in terms of money. The value of everything, from real estate, to commodities, to personal, corporate or government owned property however is not fixed. Values are in fact volatile expectations of worth. These expectations are held, not in a vault, not in a computer, not in a quarry, but in the minds of human beings. People make things, every thing valuable.

The values of all things are determined by the wants and needs, by the desires of human beings. A thing, piece of property, possession, or service is only as valuable as what a person will do, give up, trade, or pay for it. All values, all value, are set by human needs, wants or desires. And nothing "no thing" is more valuable than other people.

Needs, wants, or desires constitute demand. Human beings provide motivation, knowledge and labor to satisfy all types of demands; they create supply. The energy of ideas; thought alone, or combined by labor with natural resources, temporarily satisfies insatiable desires. Other people make it all possible. They produce what we want; they make and provide what we need. We relate to these people, we live with these people, and we rely on these people. Our economic life, even in a money system is all about relationships. Within a money system however, it is quite easy to depersonalize relationships.

Pressing on, we uncover something more profound. Desires themselves are wants and needs ultimately seeking fulfillment in feeling. Everything of value, every desire, want or need, whether it be a tangible, physical thing, a service or action, or the contemplation of an idea, leads back to a feeling. Everything we want, need or desire leads ultimately to a feeling. We human beings are meant to, are designed to, and just want to **feel**.

No one is an island unto himself. In impersonal economic terms, the terms our system of money engenders, people benefit from the time, energy and talent others apply to production, distribution, and the myriad of other value-adding pursuits to sustain and improve our quality of life. People create, attract, and supply products and services to satisfy wants and needs. People, through what they do, what they produce and what they consume, convert feelings.

The energy of desire creates or attracts circumstances to generate feelings. The economic system we use to organize society serves the same ultimate purpose: it allows us to feel; engaging in economic exchange generates feelings. We human beings are intent on changing how we feel. We are after feelings. And our most powerful feelings are those connecting us one to another. We relate, we exchange goods and services and we feel.

## Money as Proxy

Money, in the tangible medium of exchange sense, is what we collectively determine to be impersonal, quantifiable value. We value only what we want, need or desire.

The commodity of money is a creative invention of the human mind; a collective social compact made possible by our ability to abstractly accord value to symbols and infer trust to agreements. Money is a symbol representing the value of things: goods and services. We value money; an intangible idea, a function of collective trust; for what we can convert money into: feelings. Commodity money serves as a proxy for what we can have, what we can do, and for many, what we can become; ultimately for how we feel.

To attribute value to in any commodity or proxy; a paper bank note, a gold coin, a credit card, a bank account or a contract; requires the consent of both the individual user and the community. Money exists because of, and has evolved as a product of, human relationships: of trust. Money allows us to launder trust. With money we don't have to trust any specific individual and or group. As long as the majority of people collectively trust in the commodity or unit of account of whatever we call money, the system of economic exchange functions.

Money, no matter how we think of it, has individual psychological as well as social dimensions.

Any and everything only has value relative to a human being's desires. If no one wants a product or service or relationship for that matter, that object or service or relationship has no value; that object or service or relationship is worthless. Money is and only exists as an idea of relative value. Money, in theory, is as abstract and intangible as what it represents is real and tangible.

Money represents stuff; things. However, money represents something more; more influential, more desirable, and more important than stuff.

Throughout history human beings have sought to exert some measure of control on the meager circumstances of their lives. Today we still seek to gain some stability; some security in what we have come to believe is a dangerous, unstable world. This world is a dynamic, ever changing environment. Most people on the roller-coaster of life, long for power over their bodies, the environment and other people. After the need to survive the most pervasive force in the human psyche is the drive to power. We simply want to be in control and we want to be powerful.

Once human beings started to settle down and agriculture began to dominate social life property came to be synonymous with power. The more property one controlled, whether in the form of land, animals, wives, or slaves the more power one had. People, collectively, in small groups, and through governments, by agreement or by force, have gone to great lengths to secure property rights. Virtually nothing has been so contested, nor in a way sacred, as the rights to, or control over, property, in all its forms.

As the concept of money evolved; substituting agreements of value for things; money became a substitute for power. *Money, power, property* have evolved as a series of surrogates. With power the primordial desire, and survival in a material world the paramount concern, things: objects, property and possessions, became proxy for power. Over time, as we have seen, money became a proxy for things. The desire for power, for its part, springs from a natural instinct to stabilize an unstable existence. Money, that shared value, that collective trust, has come to be what we covet most. Money is power.

The idea "money is power" seems painfully dismissive of any and all higher callings, longings, and any other value. We are simple, relatively small and powerless creatures making our way in a material existence. We judge our surroundings and our success by what we see, hear, touch, taste, and smell; this is after all a physical world. And in this physical world we see limited resources, limited time, and lots of competition. We have come to believe, by lifetimes of physical evidence, that survival and success depend on the ability to compete for a share of the resource pie; to accumulate what we can, and thereby achieve some level of power over our existence. Unfortunately too many believe that in order to make it we must take it.

We can take money or we can make money. Either way, all we must do is learn the means. Before we get to means however, let's get to the heart of the issue. Why we want money.

Money is a proxy for value; things we value. Money is a proxy for products and services. And money is a proxy for power. But it isn't money or things or power any of us are really after. The end we are after is a feeling; we ultimately want to feel: we want to feel good, we want to feel secure and we want to feel happy. Money is only worth something, and the money system is only useful if it leads to or sets the conditions for human happiness.

## The Potential Energy of Trust

One could say the miracle of money is that it offers a means to level the playing field. Money is impersonal; skin color, ethnicity, religion, physical stature, social status, origin, even intellectual capacity, do not matter. Money takes all of those factors out of the economic equation. One who aspires to advance just has to be willing to engage; to make money one has to be willing to trade in trust.

The curse of money however, is that it offers a means to stack the deck, to exploit, to cheat, and to take advantage. Money is impersonal. It is faceless and nameless. It has no conscience and no personal relationships. Money has no code of conduct, does not conform to prescribed ethics and does not adhere to social conventions, a moral authority or productive principles of human relations. Taking money is as easy as exploiting trust.

For those willing to play the money game; whether by collaborating to create and share value; or by competing to take what they can; virtually anything is possible. Money is a seductive, powerful mistress.

Peeling back the onion we gain an even more profound understanding of what money really is. Money is a social construct made possible by trust. People trust other people. They trust people to do something. On the other side of trust, money represents what people do.

Money is not what makes the world go round; nor is money what makes goods and services and people go round the world. People do. People make the world go round.

Make a leap with me.

To convert a feeling, a want, need or desire, into another feeling requires energy. This conversion process from want, need or desire to a new feeling is accomplished through the expenditure of energy. In the case of an individual; an individual feels a desire and seeks to satisfy that craving. He or she must expend energy to accomplish the task of changing how he or she feels. Anything beyond the personal act of satisfying a craving requires energy from another source. People produce goods and services; people satisfy wants and needs by what they do, by committing energy. The entire process of converting feelings depends on what people do.

Products and services are expressions of energy; expressions we value. Money then, as our store of value and medium of exchange, is a store of energy. Money is potential energy.

We give money value. We tend to think what we value is things, stuff, but what we really value is feeling. Feelings are a product of energy. Money is trust; trust in some medium of exchange; some commodity or credit or debit we believe will generate some future satisfaction; some feeling. Money is an impersonal, intermediary device storing energy.

Money is potential energy.    Money is the potential energy of trust:  the currency of trust.  Money is never an end, it is always a means.  And to that means we turn next.

## Panning for Gold

- People are the key component of the social system of money.

- Human beings establish value.  Wants and needs, desires, determine value. Desire constitutes demand. To satisfy desires people create supply.

- Fundamentally an economic system is about relationships.  However, a money system allows relationships to be less personal.

- Experience is about feeling.  Supply and demand; satisfying desires is a process of converting feelings.

- Money is a proxy for what people can have, do or become.

- Money is a social compact; an instrument of trust.

- After survival the most pervasive force in the human psyche is the drive for power and money is power.

- Money is useful only if it leads to happiness.

- Money is energy, the currency of trust.

# CHAPTER 4

# A MEANS TO AN END

## Money only has the value we give it.

## Money to Happiness

Human society functions on trust. We human beings are social by nature. We need other people and other people need us. Organizing around money, like we do now, is not the only way to order society. But money and a money system offer distinct advantages.

Money serves as a proxy; a psychological store of value. We equate money with all the things money can buy and in turn all the feelings those things elicit. Money possesses an almost magical allure because of the power it possesses; the power we give it collectively. Money contains, embodies, the potential energy of trust; and for the most part it isn't even real; it is digits, a series of symbols in an account.

But money is not required to unleash, nor is it the only way to unlock the potential energy of trust. Money is not even the most popular way to unleash or unlock the potential energy of trust. Personal motivation and personal relationships are still the most common and most prevalent means of employing potential energy. We still trust those closest to us: family members, friends, colleagues and neighbors, to meet our wants and needs, some tangible and many intangible. We don't need money to enliven that trust.

Collectively however, we put money at the center of economic life. For society to work, for us to get what we want and need, people must create and produce. We trust that people will create and produce. Through a system of mutual trust people around the globe do create and produce. People solve all sorts of problems, they provide all types of services, and through their efforts they satisfy practically every want and need. Even though it isn't necessarily the only way, many of us have determined money is the best way to satisfy most if not all our wants, needs and desires.

Simple wants, complex needs, however we slice them, generate an endless array of desires. We are desire generating machines and we are always looking to satisfy those desires. We want to feel better. We always want to feel good. We want, if we can to feel great. We want to feel as good as we can for as long as we can; we call that, feeling happy. And because we often think power and status lead ultimately to happiness we attribute to that thing, that thing we believe will give us power and status, the greatest value of all. To some, money is everything; money is happiness.

## A Social Construct

Many equate power and status with happiness and therefore assume that money is the means to happiness. But all that power, all that potential energy, all that trust in money, is still just a social construct. Money only has the value we give it. Money only has value if and when we, collectively, say it does. We still must trust. We must trust the system. We must trust those who influence and manage the system. And we must trust each other.

When we lose that trust; when we lose confidence in the system or in one another, money loses value. And if our social system is organized around money, the collective "we" loses as well.

Money holds the power of potential energy. That potential energy is trust in the drive, insights, and efforts of other people. Because of what money represents many people make money their most compelling desire. These people, and that is most, believe with money they can do, have, and be anything. But the energy of trust contained in money is just potential; it is potential energy. The energy really resides with and in people. Potential energy in the form of money only exists if people collectively make it so. People make money by creating value and transferring trust. And trust, though it is a powerful force, is perishable.

Trust can be lost. Trust can be squandered. Trust can be betrayed. The more people take it; the more people abuse trust, the less likely trust is to endure. This is true in personal relationships and this is true for the collective status of money. Money is a social compact based on trust. If we misuse, misallocate and squander the collective trust in money, then money and the system of money, will not endure.

We, each of us, have at our fingertips potential energy. We can convert that potential energy into virtually anything. We can make money. Playing on a level playing field we can employ our assets to earn what we want, do what we want and become what we want. And we can help and allow others to do the same. This is what making money is all about.

On the other hand, we can decide to turn our energy to taking money. We can focus our efforts on competing and coercing, on demanding and dominating. We can choose to take instead of make. When we choose to take money instead of make it however, we risk destroying the social compact. We risk destroying trust. The more of us who decide to take it instead of make it, the more our economic system is put at risk.

## To Get What We Want

Money represents many things to many people. It is stuff, products and services. It is power. It is potential energy. It is a social compact, a social technology upon which to organize society. Money is a powerful collective tool. But money is never an end. Money is always and only a means. Money is a means to get what we want. Money is a means for all of us to get what we want; not just you, not just me; all of us.

So just what is it we are after?

The component elements of markets or whole economies for that matter are: motivation and labor, ideas and information, and physical resources. Economic pundits often focus erroneously on the tangible elements of the economic equation (physical resources) when it is the intangible elements (motivation and labor, ideas and information) that really matter.

Physical, real, tangible resources sustain living things. That is how the natural world, the physical environment functions. Nothing happens in our human economic system however, from production and distribution, to services or trade, without motivation. Motivation is the feeling of desire converted into the energy of action. Someone individually or people acting together must do something to produce or provide a product or service. A motive, a human motive, energizes people to act to meet a specific need.

The dance of supply and demand is commonly described as a physical, mechanical function. Actually the workings of supply and demand, production and consumption are physical, material and tangible as well as mental, emotional and intangible. The system we drive and are driven by is both simple and complex. It is much more than purely mechanical.

# CHAPTER 4: A MEANS TO AN END

More than a process of combining physical resources through labor, every human activity, the development of every product or service offered for trade, is the result of motivation, ideas, and information. People are intrinsically motivated to act. Desire drives action. People manipulate physical resources to fashion all means of viable products and services for personal use or trade. The more vision and insight people apply to creating products or providing services, or to improving processes, the more efficient and effective the economic supply channel becomes. The more efficient and effective the supply system, the more human wants and needs are met. The more human wants and needs are met the more trust grows and the more energy is stored in money. And the more energy is stored in money the more potential energy can be released causing people to create more.

Money is really not a store of value. Human beings create, store and represent value.

With and within human beings reside demand (desire) knowledge (know-how), and energy (unleashed as labor) to produce and provide; to supply the products and services satisfying wants and needs. Human beings have intrinsic value. People are what we trust. Money is just a convenient, artificial way to transfer trust. Human beings do not just function within or depend upon the economy, human beings *are* the economy.

Human beings' ability individually and collectively to create is unlimited. Our world economy, facilitated by the social construct of money, while by no means perfect, is evidence of humanity's ability to desire, cooperate, and create.

People need and want products and services to survive and thrive. People also create, produce and provide products and services, to satisfy demand.  Creating, producing and providing are feeling endeavors.  People are the economic engine, the economic fuel, and the economic drivers determining both supply and demand.

We feel when we create and produce and we feel when we consume.  We desire to both create and enjoy the fruits of creation.  We create, we consume, and in creating and consuming we feel.  It is feelings we ultimately are after.

People make money, earn money, empower money and take money.  People convert the energy of trust into things, into feelings.  People are the makers and mistresses of markets.

To make money, facilitate the release of potential energy.  To make money, to receive what you want or desire, first give of yourself and create.  Enliven creative energy within yourself and others to produce and provide something of value.  Making money is the process of converting energy from one form to another.  Making money is a process of creation.

To amass a fortune, seek to understand people's wants and needs, their desires, then satisfy them.  Help people get what they want.  When you do, they will transfer their trust to you.  Understanding people, at times innocently simple and at times maddeningly complex people, is the key to making money.  Giving people what they want is the key to the science of making money.

We all want our desires fulfilled.  We all want to feel and we all want to feel great.  People desire, people create; people, not money, make the world go round.

Sounds easy enough: to make money unleash energy; create or add value.  To get what you want, help people get what they want. Money is always a means to that end.

We turn to the process of creating value next.

## Panning for Gold

- Money is a psychological store of value. Money is intangible; most often it is a series of digits on account.

- Money is not the only way to enliven trust. Personal relationships are still essential.

- Though money is not the only way, many people have determined money is the best way to get what they want.

- Since people can buy virtually anything, many people believe money can buy happiness, and therefore money is happiness.

- The system, an economic system, a system of money, only works to the degree people trust in it and in each other. The real power of money, the currency of trust, resides in the energy of people.

- Money is always and only a means to an end. That end is a new feeling. Money is a means to help people feel.

- Since people put so much trust in money, money itself becomes the motive to act; the means to unleash creative human energy.

- Human beings are the economy. Money is a convenient artificial way to transfer trust. An economy still depends on people; people doing something.

- Making money is the process of generating energy; unleashing potential energy, adding value and helping people convert feelings: satisfy wants and needs.

- To amass wealth help other people get what they want. When you help others get what they want, those people will transfer trust to you.

- To master the science of making money learn what people want and how relationships work.

# PART 2

# LET'S GET DOWN TO BUSINESS

An economy is a dynamic social system facilitated by money. The system itself is powered by people attempting to satisfy desires and change how they feel. The process of satisfying desires moves money and markets. Every business is a "people business". Businesses use the energy of ideas, labor and physical materials to generate feelings. To make money, lots of money, requires the use of leverage; that leverage too, is the power of people.

# CHAPTER 5

# EMPIRE BUILDING

## Gain, save and give all you can.

## Make Your Own Way

While the Rothschild's amassed vast wealth using money to facilitate other men's ambitions, an American dynasty was built by leveraging the intangible currency of trust for decidedly tangible purposes. John Davison Rockefeller amassed the greatest fortune in history employing insightful vision, a penchant for hard work and the tenacity of conviction. He leveraged the value people ascribed to money to shape an industrial empire the likes of which the world had never seen. For Rockefeller money was a means to create something of value. Late in life Rockefeller wrote:

*I was early taught to work as well as play,*

*My life has been one long, happy holiday;*

*Full of work and full of play—*

*I dropped the worry on the way—*

*And God was good to me every day.*

The second of six children Rockefeller was the oldest son born to William Avery "Big Bill" Rockefeller, a fun-loving, vagabond snake oil salesmen and philanderer. Big Bill eventually abandoned the Rockefeller family, changed his name and started a new life in Canada. Rockefeller's mother was the force that held the family together. She was a hard-working, devout Baptist. Frugal by nature and by necessity; she taught young David the value of thrift and the grace of charity. She lived the example: *Everything you get in life is a gift from God so share it.* Rockefeller set aside no less than ten percent of his income for church and charity his entire life. Another valuable pearl of wisdom Rockefeller gleaned from his mother, "Willful waste makes woeful want." Rockefeller took this sentiment to heart; he hated to waste anything and worked diligently to ensure all his ventures operated as efficiently and effectively as humanly possible.

Rockefeller was an industrious child. As the oldest son of a father who was rarely seen, young Rockefeller shouldered the burden of regular household chores. He recognized early on what needed to be done. He earned money selling potatoes and candy to other children and raised and sold turkeys for his mother. He contributed to family finances as needed and still managed to save a tidy sum. On the advice of his mother he lent some of his savings to trustworthy neighbors. When the money he lent was returned to him with interest he began to understand that it was better to let money serve rather than become a slave to money.

In the 1840's and 50's pursuing opportunities to the west Big Bill relocated the Rockefeller clan a few times in central New York. Finally, pushing farther west, he settled the family in Cleveland, Ohio. Young Rockefeller, when he got the opportunity, proved to be a disciplined and serious student. His favorite subject, and the one he demonstrated the greatest talent for was mathematics. He attended two years of high school in Cleveland and then completed a ten-week business training program where he mastered accounting and bookkeeping among other business disciplines.

In 1855, at the age of 16, after some diligent job hunting, Rockefeller secured a position as an assistant bookkeeper with a small produce commission firm there in Cleveland. The firm bought, shipped, and sold agricultural commodities on commission. Rockefeller was not earning big money, fifty cents a day, but he loved his work. He reveled over every aspect of the business. He worked hard, proving himself to be exacting, tenacious and exceedingly honest. He earned the trust of his employer and his customers, and he began building a reputation for getting things done amongst the wider business community.

Rockefeller's first real job was such an opportunity, for the rest of his life he celebrated September 26th, his first day on the job "job day" like most people celebrate their birthdays. That first job was the break launching him into the business world where he grew and prospered personally and professionally. That job was the beginning of an amazing career and an extraordinary life.

Though Big Bill Rockefeller had preferred a life unshackled by responsibility he had taught his son some worthwhile life lessons. Rockefeller learned from his father to strive to get the best deal possible and for the most part that was only likely if and when you were in control of your own destiny or at least calling the shots. After a few years as a trusted, hard-working employee, learning everything he could about retailing, wholesaling and the shipping business Rockefeller decided to take a calculated risk and venture out on his own.

In 1859 Rockefeller partnered with a neighbor Maurice Clark. Together they raised $4,000 in capital and opened their own produce commission business. Rockefeller applied his commercial acumen to the very competitive business of buying, shipping and selling agricultural products and other commodities. In a highly competitive, low-margin business Rockefeller saw ways to improve efficiencies others had not. The first year in business the pair grossed $450,000 and turned a profit. With the outbreak of the Civil War commodity prices rose, this in turn boosted shipping commissions. The next year in business the pair did even better. The business grew year over year.

Rockefeller traveled untiringly, drumming up business throughout the Lake Erie region. He was thorough and precise in his dealings with customers, suppliers, and transporters. He borrowed money to continually expand operations but never speculated or gave advances on loans. Using money as leverage Rockefeller was on his way to becoming a wealthy man.

A committed abolitionist, during the Civil War Rockefeller supported Abraham Lincoln and the Republican Party, but he chose to keep his focus on business rather than politics. With all his hard work and travels Rockefeller realized the prospects for agricultural commerce were limited in Cleveland. Other regions of the northern Midwest had advantages Cleveland lacked. In August 1859 the first oil well ever drilled set off an oil frenzy in northwestern Pennsylvania. Rockefeller saw another opportunity.

Oil refining was not a capital intensive business. The financial barriers to entry were low, but the market was heating up. Whale oil was in short supply and was getting ever more expensive. Crude oil could provide light, but it also could be put to many more uses. The industry as a whole was in its infancy. More uses for oil were being discovered every day. The oil men were just "figuring it out"; production, refining, distribution; all of it. This was an industry that could benefit from business smarts, organizational skills, and a proclivity for efficiency. Oil was right in John D. Rockefeller's wheel-housing. This was an industry tailored for his expertise.

## But Don't Go It Alone

Rockefeller understood the power of collaboration. He collaborated extensively throughout his business career. No man can succeed in business by himself. It takes a team, a talented group of individuals working together to achieve anything worthwhile. Rockefeller determined to select the teams. Rockefeller and Clark found a chemist, Samuel Andrews, who knew how to refine oil. Along with Clark's two brothers, the five men established a refinery: Andrews, Clark & Company, in Cleveland.

The Pennsylvania crude was high quality oil. Two thirds of it could yield kerosene for lamps another ten percent or so could be refined into useful chemicals but the remainder was considered waste. Rockefeller abhorred waste so he devoted considerable effort to improving the efficiency of operations from wellhead to refining to distribution to final use. Rockefeller attended to every detail. He vertically integrated operations, going so far as to establish his own barrel making facilities, complete with woodlots for providing raw materials and fuel and a fleet of wagons and horses to transport what resources the refinery required.

Over the initial two years of operations Rockefeller's vision for growth started to diverge from that of the Clark brothers. The Clark brothers did now want to borrow money to expand. Rockefeller was convinced borrowing money was the way to grow so as to ultimately dominate the oil industry. At the ripe old age of 24 Rockefeller bought out the Clark brothers for $72,500 and gained complete control of oil operations. Rockefeller then brought in his younger brother William and expanded. Together they further increased efficiencies in all aspects of the firm. They borrowed heavily and plowed all profits back into expansion.

The oil industry was ultra-competitive and growing fast. Rockefeller realized he had to add value everywhere he could and stay ahead of or drive the commodity growth curve as much as possible. Breaking his teeth in the competitive world of agricultural commodities Rockefeller was uniquely positioned to influence the growth and maturing of the petroleum industry. But to ensure things went his way he had to make some bold moves swiftly.

In 1866 the Rockefeller brothers built another refinery in Cleveland. This one they called Standard Works. They also opened an export office in New York which William ran. Oil exports eventually outgrew domestic distribution and proved extremely profitable.

## Collaborate or Compete

Men with the intellect, insight and foresight to partner with John D. Rockefeller grew very, very rich. Those who decided to compete against him went broke. With an eye toward efficiency Rockefeller was an adherent of the Darwinian philosophy of business: *survival of the fittest*. Rockefeller had relationships with railroad men and ferry operators; he had relationships with financiers and merchants. He collaborated with the people who made things happen and he leveraged those relationships to monopolize an industry.

With the Civil War satisfactorily concluded the industrial might of the nation turned toward reconstruction and the rapid exploitation of new technologies and fledgling industries; most notably railroads and oil. The Rockefellers brought on a new partner, Henry Flagler, and continued to aggressively expand operations. They borrowed money wisely, reinvested profits, controlled costs up and down the refining and distribution chain, and they creatively found new uses for what most competing refiners considered waste. Rockefeller made sure his margins were better than all competitors.

In June of 1870, Rockefeller, as majority shareholder, and his partners formed Standard Oil. With the backing of all the major banks in the region Standard Oil went on a buying spree to acquire any competition. Rockefeller assessed competing operations. He offered a fair price in Standard Oil stock if the competing owners were amenable to joining him or in cash if not. If a competing firm refused Rockefeller's offer that firm soon felt the brunt of shrewd strategies designed to drive that firm out of the oil business. Standard Oil could cut prices and sustain a long term price war or, because of their clout with the railroads and the financiers, could drive up transportation and borrowing cost. Or they could attack competitors virtually any and everywhere along the distribution chain. Few organizations could withstand Standard Oil.

Standard Oil gobbled up oil refiners and petroleum related companies at an astonishing rate. Soon Rockefeller was the most profitable petroleum refiner in Ohio. Exploiting tactics that worked Standard Oil quickly became one of the largest, fully integrated petroleum producers, refiners and distributors in the world.

John D. Rockefeller loved every minute of the adventure; building the enterprise. He labored, from his perspective, to empower and fuel the nation and the world. By doing so he became the richest man on earth.

At one point Rockefeller controlled nearly ninety percent of the petroleum industry. Eventually competitors and politicians alike become convinced that a monopoly did not serve the public interest. Though Rockefeller believed in an industry such as oil, the name of the game was efficiency, and the greatest efficiency could only be had by vertical and horizontal integration to manage supply, streamline distribution, and ultimately control costs. While in theory a monopoly offers certain efficiencies it also inherently presents significant opportunities for abuse; tremendous risk. Standard Oil was eventually broken into over thirty separate and distinct companies. Rockefeller however, maintained an interest in all of them. He grew wealthier than ever.

By his late 50's John D. Rockefeller was feeling the wear and tear of empire building. He retired from active management of his business holdings. His long time business partners took more active roles in the companies and together they brought on other professional managers to continue expansion. Rockefeller had had five children, four daughters and a son, John Junior eventually took over management of the family fortune from his father.

John D. Rockefeller spent forty years in retirement. He devoted his energy primarily to philanthropic pursuits. He founded universities, financed medical centers and eradicated disease; he funded church missions and supported the arts. In total he gave away more than $530 million to various causes. Both his fortune and his philanthropy would be valued in the hundreds of billions of dollars today.

From humble beginnings, using the insight of ideas, the vitality of action, and the leverage of the currency of trust John D. Rockefeller made money on a monumental scale. One man's ambition, coupled with an unprecedented opportunity reshaped the world. John D. Rockefeller built a business by collaborating and competing. He intended to make things better and to do things better than his competitors could. By wasting not, he wanted not. In his life John D. Rockefeller gained as much as he could, saved as much as he could, and gave away as much as he could. Money was not what he was after; it was just a way for others to keep score.

## Panning for Gold

- Everything you get in life is a gift from God, share it.

- Do what needs to be done.

- Let money serve you rather than become a slave to money.

- Learn all you can.

- Earn trust by working hard and being exacting, tenacious and honest.

- Take control of your own destiny.

- Collaborate with trustworthy, capable people.

- Leverage money intelligently.

- Be willing to change direction if opportunities arise.

- Add value wherever you can.

- Conserve value and improve efficiencies where possible.

- Give as much as you can.

# CHAPTER 6

# THE MONEY-GO-ROUND

## People make the money go round.

## From Theory to Practice

Money is not what most people think it is. We define money as: a medium of exchange, a unit of account, and a store of value. If we go a step farther we say money is all that plus really money is a social technology, a system allowing people to track and transfer credits and debts, assets and liabilities. What we are really talking about is a social compact, a dynamic system of energy in motion; what could be called the money-go-round.

Money represents potential energy: the potential energy of trust between people. Money is the currency of trust.

That all sounds well and good in theory, but the Rothschild's and Rockefellers were not theorists. The Rothschild's amassed a fortune trading in trust and John D. Rockefeller leveraged the power of money to build an oil empire; how is this theory of money put to practical use?

Let's begin by gaining some perspective.

How much money is out there? Where is it? Who controls it? And, what makes the money go round?

Though, as we have seen money can be a difficult concept to pin down. For our concrete purposes here, we can use standard measures for what economists call the money supply.  The U.S. monetary base, comprised of currency in circulation or held at banks, totals approximately $4 Trillion. Beyond currency, coins and notes, the workable "money supply" consists of "relatively" liquid instruments and assets routinely used to facilitate the exchange of goods and services.  The current value of currency, deposit accounts, and special instruments, what economists consider "M2", is $11.6 Trillion (that's a lot of zeros: $11,600,000,000,000.00).  This is the money we, in the United States use, to conduct business.

To pull us out of the stratosphere, let's break the money supply figure down a bit.  At the beginning of 2015 the U.S. population stood at about 320 million persons (the global population was approximately 7.3 billion people). On a per capita basis, the U.S. money supply of $11.6 Trillion amounts to $36,250.00 circulating in currency or on account, for every man, woman, and child in America.  And this "M2" doesn't include the big stuff: large time-deposits, money market accounts or other substantial liquid assets.

How much money is in your pocket and in your accounts?  How are you doing as a household?  Multiply the number of people in your household by $36k; is that what you have stuffed in your mattress or on account?

The money supply, examined from this perspective however, is just a static instrument.  In reality money, like people and like energy, is always in motion; it is transferring from one hand to another, from one credit account to another.

The United States has the largest single economy in the world, an economy on par with the entire economy of the European Union.  The U.S. gross domestic product (GDP) for 2014, the market value of all goods and services produced, was approximately $17.4 Trillion.  The European

Union's GDP for 2014 is estimated to have been $18.4 Trillion. China, with the next largest single economy, had an estimated 2014 GDP of $10.4 Trillion. The world GDP for 2014 was on the order of $73 Trillion.

To personalize these numbers, consider this: if we equalized output to a per person basis, every man, women and child in the United States would have produced approximately $54,375.00 worth of goods and services in 2014. We know all things aren't equal; but, if the nation produced $54k worth of value for each person last year, how much did you make?

How did your household fare? The economy generated $54 thousand worth of value per person. Multiply the $54k by the number of working adults in your household. Did you bring in that much? Interestingly enough the median household income in the United States in 2014 was just shy of $54,000.00; as many households brought in more than $54k that year as brought in less. How much of the "value added" produced in the United States in 2014 flowed through your hands?

It's not fair to invoke averages. Averages are the tools of statisticians. As one man astutely observed, "The average human has one breast and one testicle." Don't be upset if you aren't meeting the averages. This illustration is meant to give you a sense for the quantity of dollars out there to be had; dollars that can just as easily pass through your hands as anyone else's.

## What We Value

The U.S. money supply and GDP are pretty impressive numbers, but that's not the half of it. Consider the financial or monetary value of all the stuff in America: all the real property, plant and equipment, products of all kinds, financial assets and intellectual property, ideas and knowledge.  Economists have calculated the value of real stuff in the United States amounts to about $112 Trillion. And we are part of a globalized economy of much greater value.  And of course this isn't all the assets people are working with.  When the time-value of financial assets are included, credit markets and the markets comprised of derivatives of all sorts worldwide are approaching sums exceeding a quadrillion dollars.

The scope of these numbers is impressive, but largely irrelevant.  They do however; tell us there are lots of opportunities out there; lots of value already in existence, and lots of opportunity to add value.  Let's ratchet our discussion back down to the reality most of us live and breathe; the reality we operate in and can influence.

We have discussed "estimated values"; what things are worth.  Something, anything, is only worth what someone will pay for it.  The value of a car, a house, clothes, furniture, and labor is only worth what some person will give for it. Nothing in this world is static.  The concept of value too, what something is worth, is dynamic.  Things change. Assigning value to anything assumes a degree of risk.  What one person holds dear others may not consider valuable at all.  Value is a guess, often an educated guess as to what other people will agree to.

**People determine value.**  People determine value and they determine value in relation to other people through relationships.

In the context of money and wealth, if we were to ask people what they value, most would point to stuff: the house, the car, property and possessions.  Like we discussed previously, most people think of wealth in material terms.  If we peel back the onion, if we throw open the curtain we discover what people really value even in the context of money and wealth. People value freedom and comfort, status and power: intangible things. People ultimately value feelings.

Life is a feeling-action-feeling adventure: we feel, we act, and then we feel again. A quest for fame, fortune and glory starts and ends the same way a quest for privacy and comfort starts and ends: with feelings.

Making money and taking money start from the same impulse: a feeling to move, to do something, to become something, to change something. That impulse is the urge to realize another feeling. Having money, being wealthy is not about temporarily possessing something representing power; having money and being wealthy are about feeling powerful, feeling important, feeling comfortable and feeling free. People want to have more, do more and be more; they want to feel more; and for many, having money or being wealthy makes those opportunities to feel possible.

What do people value? People value feelings; some feelings very much more than others.

## Round and Round It Goes

People's wants and needs, their desires are virtually limitless. It is wants and needs, desires, "feelings" which move us to act. Our actions, the actions of human beings produce all the stuff and provide all the labor we categorize as the trappings of wealth.

We feel something; we act. We produce; we create value. Then we provide that value to other people who are attempting to meet wants and needs, who are intending to satisfy desires. People produce the value, the material, the products and the services which help people feel the way they want to feel. People simply want to change how they feel. Markets help people change their feelings.

An economy is not a nameless, faceless impersonal market. Money, an impersonal medium of exchange, allows us to pretend that a market is detached and separate from human beings, "It's just business." but it never really is. A market, an economy, generates value, amasses value, and provides value only when people do. People determine value.

Value, measured in money, is a function of satisfying wants and needs, fulfilling desires. The value of all things is determined by human begins' feelings: wants and needs, desires. Opportunities exist for making money by creating value. People who produce things or add value by what they do fulfill wants and needs. By fulfilling wants and needs, by satisfying desires, by helping other people get what they want producers and providers secure for themselves immense value.

In economic terms, value is set by demand: a sense of lack, need, desire or want. Supply is also determined by demand: a sense of lack, need, desire or want. Supply and demand are the outcome of the motivation to act, the human motivation to survive, to create and to thrive.

Human beings provide the motivation, the knowledge, and the labor to meet all types of economic demands; wants and needs. People need and want, and to the degree they need and want, people determine value. People also produce, they supply; they fulfill demand. People are the economic engine, the economic fuel, and the economic drivers. People are the key to understanding the money-go-round.

Nothing happens in terms of production, distribution, services or trade without the motivation to act "labor" and ideas or knowledge. Someone, or increasingly some interdependent group, must do something to produce or provide a product or service meeting any and every want or need. The dance of supply and demand is a vast human undertaking.

The single greatest stores of value; knowledge, know-how, labor, motivation; all the feelings of supply and demand, are possessed by and are in human beings. Human beings have monetary value. In the final analysis, the monetary value of human beings dwarfs the estimated value of all the stuff, all the property and possessions we normally equate with wealth. People make money, people earn money, and people empower money: **People make the money-go-round.**

*People make the money-go-round* is the key realization for anyone who aspires to riches. People have desires, then focus energy to realize those desires. Money and markets are a means to facilitate this process. Understanding and serving people is the path to prosperity. Making money is fundamentally about adding value, about adding value by helping people. Making money means contributing to life, helping life grow, helping the energy of life flow. By serving people, by satisfying wants and needs, by fulfilling desires people make money.

## Panning for Gold

- The U.S. money supply is comprised of nearly $12 Trillion.

- Money represents "potential energy" when held and "kinetic energy" when employed.

- The U.S. economy produced about $17.4 Trillion worth of goods and services in 2014.

- Value is not fixed or static; it changes.

- People determine value.

- People ultimately value feelings. Any and every thing is only a means to convert feelings.

- Life is a feeling-action-feeling process.

- Wants and needs, desires, are virtually limitless.

- The processes of production, distribution and consumption; what makes markets and economies; are all a means to convert feelings.

- Value, as measured by money, is a function of satisfying wants and needs: fulfilling desires; converting feelings.

- Making money is creating value to convert feelings.

- Supply and demand are set by a sense of lack. This sense of lack is a motive to act.

- Human beings are the economy. People make the money go round.

- Understanding and serving people, fulfilling desires, is the way to prosperity.

# CHAPTER 7

# TIME TRAVELS & POWER SURGES

**I know they were here; they left something valuable behind.**

## The People Business

We are all in the people business. If you prefer to be more exacting you might say we are all in the "feelings" business. Trade and commerce, production and distribution, the business of business is all about people: people's wants and needs, people's desires, people's feelings. Money is made by satisfying wants and needs, by fulfilling desires; by helping people get what they want; by helping people change how they feel. It's as simple as that.

Every aspect of life is interpreted as feeling. Life is all about feelings. Business is about changing feelings, but not everything in life is business. Most of what generates feelings has nothing to do with trade, commerce, production, distribution or consumption. Relationships, connecting with and relating to other people and managing those connections dominates the realm of feelings. Living is primarily about relating and relationships. But in a material or consumption-oriented society, like we have in the United States and increasingly around the world, business is a prime mover.

Human beings are social by nature. The family is the building block of human society. Families band together in tribes and clans and communities. Societies evolve as a means of protection and survival and ultimately as a means to grow and thrive. Over thousands of years and despite much conflict we have, for the most part, realized we are better off cooperating and collaborating to get what we want. We are better off working together. Business is one way to work together, to create and connect; and provide for every conceivable want and need.

An individual can be in business for themselves, but they can't go it alone. No one can go it alone. To survive and to thrive people require the benefits of community: the knowledge, the tools, the infrastructure and the labor others provide. Since business is by its very nature a creative social activity, grouping together to produce and distribute products or provide services offers distinct advantages.

Creating and adding value is predominantly a human undertaking. We value most what people do. Collaborating with others to create allows people to explore new perspectives and innovate. Working together motivates and inspires people. And collaborating multiplies the energy available to devote to any productive endeavor, "Many hands make light work." Working together collaboratively has the potential to generate more energy, more productive value and potentially more money, than working separately as individuals.

On the demand side of the equation human beings in aggregate have similar wants and needs. We are individuals for sure, we have our differences, but we are more alike than different. One consistent, near uniform desire is to want what other people have. Determining people's wants and needs and satisfying them is the business of business. The essence of business is changing how people feel. Those feelings are conduits for power. Feelings drive the currency of trust. Making money is about manipulating and leveraging that currency; that energy.

## Something Left Behind

Time is our most precious asset. Time is how we experience change. Time is how our perspective changes. Unfortunately time is what people squander most. We know we are alive because we feel. People feel great or feel awful or feel somewhere in between. They spend time, energy and effort pursuing great feelings or spend time, energy and effort eluding awful feelings. Or many waste time; they fritter it away attempting to avoid feeling anything at all.

People tend to think they have all the time in the world, when in reality everyone has an expiration date. We only get to feel for so long, and then it's off to something else. We have options. We can focus and use our time to create or destroy. We can use our talents and our energy to add value or to take it away. And depending on what we do, we can make the energy of our lives travel through time; we can ensure our energy endures. By what we choose to do we can leave something behind.

We tend to think of labor as an intangible quality. Labor is an action, the dispensing or employing of energy. Think of labor like electricity in a wire. Electricity is energy in motion to apply to a task; powering a piece of equipment for example. That electricity, that energy is not lost, it is transformed. Our personal energy too, like the energy of electricity, is transformed into something of value. The benefits of labor used to create things are transformed and remain as potential energy for later use. The value of labor, the energy of action, endures in what people create.

Every manmade device or natural resource that has been moved or manipulated to whatever end contains within it the remnants of some human beings' ideas, energy and efforts. The energy of that person or persons, those people or organizations or businesses, is traveling through time to assist the current user.  The energy of everyone who labors, everyone who builds, everyone who creates, travels through time for as long as that thing endures.

What you live in, what you drive, what you hold in your hand represents the residual value of human ideas and labor.  We value what people do; the energy that flows through people.

"Why does this matter?" you may ask.

Because making money is all about people: creating value and leveraging the value others create.  Understanding this point is essential to understanding how money moves and how money is made.

Every new generation builds on the past.  We rely on work conducted in the past.  We rely on the infrastructure that was built: homes and businesses, structures of all sorts; roads, bridges, railways and so on forming transportation networks; wires, cables and devices enabling communication networks; and energy distribution grids, to mention a few. All of these things, these networks and systems are evidence of enduring labor; of energy traveling through time; of residual value.

People routinely use that labor, that residual value as leverage to create.  People rely on infrastructure and technology, gadgets and gizmos, machines, devices and products of all sorts to create, produce and conduct business. People rely on the residual value of human labor.

We, all of us, take advantage of energy from past action.  We leverage the labor which endures through time. Information technology is a prime example.  Computer code written today rests upon and relies upon code written before. The energy and ideas of past code writers endure.  The actions of the past, of ideas applied and work completed, still exists in every manmade thing we rely on. What people produce (physical things) possesses the residual value of the ideas and actions of people and can be leveraged.

The ideas and energy we contribute to creating, to adding value endure. Everyone however does not leave the same mark. Everyone does not have the same influence or offer the same contribution to the future. How much one leaves behind, how much one contributes, depends on how much energy one directs and toward what ends.

Ideas and labor travel through time. The energy of thoughts and actions endure in what people create. Actions, embedded in creations, travel to be of value to others in the future. In money terms, human beings value most what other human beings do. We value creative ideas and energy people contribute. We value human action most, and we all leave something behind.

## Where Energy Surges

Everything we understand about this reality is a process of converting energy. Energy is the dynamic motion of life. Our human feeling conversion process is an energy conversion process. Human beings manipulate and direct energy in the physical world to alter their state; to experience a new feeling; to change how they feel. How much a person feels and the intensity of what they feel is a matter of connecting with and facilitating the flow of energy. How much money people make is a matter of connecting with and facilitating the flow of energy.

People live exciting and exhilarating or dull and empty lives depending on how they connect to and facilitate the flow of energy. The more "plugged in" a person is, the more energy surges through his or her life and the more opportunities he or she has to create and contribute. The more energy that flows through your life the more opportunities you have to make money.

Where energy surges opportunities abound.

To use a more familiar analogy, consider how water flows. Water is found all over the planet. Water pools together and flows in response to the forces of heat, wind and gravity. In some places it's barely a trickle but as more water gathers together it forms a raging river. Water ebbs and flows, surges and subsides. Water is a form of energy. Money, the currency of trust, also is a form of energy. Money ebbs and flows, surges and subsides too.

So, just where does money surge?

Money as a social tool responds to human forces: individual desires and collective wants and needs. Collective wants and needs constitute political power. On a macro level, in aggregate, money flows where we "collectively" want it too.

Most of the money in the U.S. economy, as measured by GDP calculations, is flowing through the government, finance, and healthcare sectors. Though not originally conceived for the purpose of redistributing wealth, the U.S. government seems to naturally have migrated to this function. Finance, in theory, is meant to support business: allocating the currency of trust to meet wants and needs through the production and distribution of real goods and services. But since we award money the preeminent power position in society, manipulating trust and taking money have become the focus of finance. Healthcare as an industry, for various reasons, has grown disproportionately to what a healthy society should need. These three segments, government, finance, and healthcare constitute over two-thirds of the U.S. economy. We collectively force most of the energy of our economy into these three streams.

Human desires drive the energy of society. Social systems, to include monetary systems, are a means to manage the process of fulfilling desires. Operating optimally a society uses money to serve the public interests, to benefit the population. However when a society erroneously attributes more value to something other than people, in this case money, money commands ultimate power. We turn the system inside out. Instead of being a tool to use to satisfy desires, a servant, money becomes master. In our energy dynamic, money as the currency of trust has become the focal point. Wherever the currency of trust is directed energy surges.

The energy of an economy is primarily human: ideas and labor (including the residual value of labor). Energy flows toward the concentration of human desires. Desires are the primary factor determining where the currency of trust and therefore human energy flows. Money is made by generating, manipulating and directing surging energy. Wherever energy surges opportunities to make money exist.

Next we explore what it is to control surging energy.

## Panning for Gold

- We are all in the people business; really the feelings business.
- Businesses make money by helping people get what they want; by changing how they feel.
- Human beings value most what human beings do.
- Collaborating to create value offers definite and distinct advantages.
- Time is our most precious asset.
- The residual value of labor, the ideas and action people contribute; endure in what those people make.
- Any thing containing the enduring value of labor offers leverage.
- Where energy surges opportunities abound.
- Money is made by generating, manipulating and directing surging energy.

# CHAPTER 8

# PULL THE LEVERS

## Keep your eye on the ball.

## The Biggest Bang

Have you noticed that about twenty percent of customers or clients generate about eighty percent of a company's revenue? Or that about twenty percent of streets back up with eighty percent of the traffic? Or, now be honest, you wear about twenty percent of your clothes eighty percent of the time?

Very few things in life are uniform, and those few things that are will surely not stay that way for long. Few things, to include energy, are rarely distributed equally. Energy is always in motion, ebbing and flowing, surging and subsiding. The natural, physical world and the social world are in constant motion, both are evolving and changing. Balance, if achieved, is only a temporary state. Imbalance is the more typical order.

There exists an inherent imbalance between causes and results, inputs and outputs, effort and reward. Some inputs produce little output while other causes produce extraordinary results. This imbalance is known as the *Pareto Principle* or more commonly the *80/20 Rule*.

The *Pareto Principle* states that eighty percent of results in business and in life stem from a mere twenty percent of efforts. Basically some things matter more. Some few things produce outsized results. Most things matter little and most causes produce few, if any, results.

The *80/20 Rule* stipulates causes or inputs come in two varieties: first the majority category, these are causes with little impact; the eighty percent. Then there is the second or minority category, these are the causes or inputs with major or dominant impact; twenty percent causes. To produce the greatest result from any effort people are best served leveraging twenty percent causes; getting the biggest bang for the buck.

Vilfredo Frederico Damaso Pareto, an Italian engineer, sociologist, economist, political scientist and philosopher, lived from 1848 to 1923. During his exploration into the fields of sociology and economics Pareto noticed a particular pattern of disparity as to who controlled the majority of wealth. He discovered that about twenty percent of the people always control about eighty percent of the wealth. Other researchers verified this ratio holds across a wide spectrum of observations in the social world of human relations as well as in the natural, physical world.

Human beings operate in, around and with, what might be termed the "vital few" and "trivial many". A few things are always more important than most things. To deliberately realize the greatest output or value determine which things are the *vital few* and which things are the *trivial many* and act accordingly.

The *80/20 Rule* stipulates, and you know this from experience, a few people add most of the value. All people are valuable and all people contribute, but when it comes to manipulating energy and making money a few people do it much better than most. We all want to be one of those few people. To experience an extraordinary level of success and to make money easily look for the twenty percent causes and employ that leverage. The next best option, if you can't figure out how to employ the twenty percent causes yourself, is to associate with those people who can.

Make the *80/20 Rule* work for you, not against you. Take control of your life. Work the levers.

## Equality Exists only in Theory

The United States was founded on the bedrock principal of equality; not to make all things equal, but rather offering equal opportunity to all. Freedom and opportunity go hand in hand. Having freedom and opportunity, some people will choose to do something and some will choose to do nothing. Some will choose to produce and others to consume. Some will choose to create and others to destroy. Some will choose to make and others to take. Equality under the law and equality of opportunity allow individuals to prosper in a free society. But human beings are not inclined to be equal.

People automatically and naturally stratify. Everyone must meet subsistence needs; after that however, people automatically and naturally focus on different things. Human beings tend to admire, respect and esteem certain traits and attributes above others. Even without money as a factor, social groups establish and maintain a social order. Some people are satisfied conforming and belonging, while others want to stand out.

Certain characteristics give people marked advantages over others without those attributes. Different social groups value certain attributes above others to varying degrees. Possessing a unique something people value gives that person a decided advantage; some leverage. Advantageous attributes include:

- Physical Prowess, Athletic Ability, Physical Skills

- Looks, Attractiveness, Beauty
- Gender
- Size and Stature mostly in relation to Physical Power and Strength
- Intelligence, Intellect, Vision, Imagination
- Artistic Talents of Expression (music, dance, acting, creating objects of expression)
- Social Graces, Communication Skills, Ability to Connect with Others

People stratify in other ways besides by personal attributes.  They stratify to varying degrees based on "mutually agreed" upon factors.  These social factors include:

- Age
- Size of Family, Number of Children
- Bloodline, Heredity
- Race / Ethnicity
- Religion
- Position / Responsibility within an organization or group
- Social Status as determined by a combination of personal and social factors
- Money and money's equivalents (property, power, control over resources and labor)

Possessing one or more of the advantaged characteristics gives an individual or group standing or status.  That person automatically occupies a position of greater esteem and status and potentially wields greater influence within the group.  That talent, skill or feature is a point of leverage. That person can access and manipulate more energy because of the influence they wield.  They have the potential to make more money.

Groups within societies tend to stratify as well. While societies stratify differently, they typically allocate social power in an 80/20 distribution. Power concentrates at the top, while the population concentrates at the bottom. Here is a typical hierarchy:

**Elites / Rulers** (people with money, power and social influence) (**upper class**)

**Warriors, Politicians, Professionals** (maintaining social order) (**middle class**)

**Merchants, Managers, Entrepreneurs** (maintaining productive order) (**middle class**)

**Workers, Laborers, Students** (**middle / working class**)

**Weak, Sick, Dependent, Needy** (**lower class**)

The human tendency to stratify and concentrate power, though formidable, is not absolute. The more free and equal a society the less power concentrates and the greater the chance for individuals to achieve social mobility. Money simplifies the social mobility equation. Since, in aggregate, people value money the most, acquiring money is the surest way to ascend the social hierarchy. While many people choose to take money; a better course is to make money.

At least eighty percent of value in any "thing" is the value of human ideas and labor. To make money the challenge is using what you have to the best of your ability. Leverage the traits and social status you enjoy to meet wants and needs; to help people get what they want. The more value you create or control, the more money you potentially can make. Gain control of some leverage and extend your influence.

## Levers and Pulleys

To make more money, create and add more value.  You create and add more value by fulfilling desires, by satisfying wants and needs; by helping people change how they feel.  The more people you help the more money you potentially make.  Or the more powerful the people you help the more money you potentially make.  To do the best you can with what you've got; to create the biggest bang possible, gain control of the most leverage.

A lever or pulley is a device which offers the user a mechanical advantage.  Employing a lever or pulley a person can exert more force than they would be able to apply directly.  To make the most money, employ the most leverage.  Use the levers and pulleys you have access to.

Consider using these points of leverage.  They each have advantages and disadvantages.  Used properly a lever or pulley will greatly multiply your efforts and effects.  Figure out how to control or influence the levers and pulleys you need to create your own fortune:

**Natural Resources, Particularly Energy**:  Natural resources are a component of all physical creations.  Natural resources typically represent "twenty percent" of the value of any thing.   However, modern society relies on energy (primarily from oil and gas, but nuclear, gravity (dams), wind, and solar sources as well) to meet virtually all survival needs.   Therefore control of sources of energy offers disproportionate leverage.

**Machinery / Technology**:  Capital equipment and devices retain the residual value of labor.  They allow whoever controls that machine or technology to leverage the ideas and actions of everyone who contributed to making that thing.  Some items offer tremendous leverage.

**Organizational Systems / Information and Communication Systems**: How a process is organized and managed and how information and ideas are managed, employed and communicated to influence action is an opportunity for leverage.

Natural resources, machinery, and systems are tangible, physical examples of leverage. Great leverage also exists in the social dimension.

**Social Order / Political Structure**: How a society organizes, the laws they abide by and the rules of the game the society applies determine how energy is managed, transferred and created. The social order offers points of leverage.

**Money**: To the degree a population empowers money; money may be the ultimate lever in human affairs. As a proxy for most anything, including the levers and pulleys listed here, money can be leveraged. The social technology of money too can be leveraged. Leveraging money is stretching the currency of trust. Government representatives and financial elites routinely manipulate money. They alter the rules regarding the standards and uses of money. They expand time horizons and shift risk. They devalue the currency by printing more. The currency of trust is a powerful lever; one that can be used for positive or negative results.

**Market Influence**: Influence is the ability to control or direct human action by manipulating desire. Marketing and advertising are the primary means of influence in free markets. Marketing and advertising is an attempt to get people to feel a certain way, to generate a desire, which will in turn stimulate an action. In a money economy, typically this means "buy" something.

**Political Influence**:  This is the concentration of social capital or social control.  Political influence maintains social order in a society.  Political influence only exists when, where, and if people agree it does.  Political influence often is misallocated and becomes a means for exerting social control; and coercive power.  Anyone exercising political influence regarding money must be careful to apply that power to making and not taking money.

**Personal Influence**:  Personal relationships, personal status, and trust can all be leveraged.  The bonds that bind people together may be used to get other people to help an individual, team or organization make money.

**Time**:  Most monetary transactions leverage time.  The ability to leverage time is one of the most advantageous characteristics of a monetary system.  However, not all time is subject to the influence of money.  Individuals, groups and organizations routinely leverage time by promising a future benefit for an action today.

Creating value is only half the money making equation. To monetize a transaction that value must be transferred to someone else.  Making money is creating and delivering value.

An individual can create and deliver value alone.  To create and deliver significant value in a competitive marketplace however requires the advantage of leverage. Leverage is most frequently a product of people: people's energy and effort now; people's energy and effort over time; or people's trust.  Find points of leverage to multiply your efforts.  Pull the levers.

## Panning for Gold

- Eighty percent of results stem from twenty percent of efforts. We are surrounded by the "vital few" and the "trivial many".

- Equality only exists in theory. Energy is always flowing; concentrating and scattering.

- People automatically and naturally stratify.

- People ascribe power to certain characteristics, traits and social factors. These can be leveraged.

- Societies, like individuals, stratify. Social power always concentrates in the hands of a few.

- A lever or pulley is a device offering a mechanical advantage. To make money find and employ points of leverage.

- Leverage is usually a product of people. Employing leverage is the process of using other people's energy, ideas, and money.

# PART 3

# THE PEOPLE BUSINESS

We are all in the people business as making money is about changing how people feel. This section of *Money, The New Science of Making It* focuses specifically on the human dimension. Please consider the ideas in this section from two perspectives: 1) A personal perspective as to how you approach life and making money; and 2) A perspective of understanding what causes people to act or not act.

# CHAPTER 9

## EMPOWERING EVERYONE

**Next time you see something new
examine it as if it is an opportunity.
Then ask yourself: Am I willing to take the risk?**

## Grabbing Hold

Is your attention drawn to shiny new objects? Do you like to try new things? Do you like a challenge? Is learning to master something new more like an adventure or a game than drudgery or a chore? If you answer yes to these questions you may have more in common with the wealthiest man in America than you thought.

William Henry Gates III, more commonly known as Bill Gates, was born October 28, 1955 in Seattle, Washington. Gates came into this world blessed with three distinct advantages: he was born to a wealthy, well-connected, supportive family; he was more intelligent and driven than most; and he arrived on the scene just as powerful innovations were blossoming. Bill Gates entered a world of opportunity. But what distinguished Gates most from all the other "rich kids" was his willingness to embrace opportunity and take a risk. Gates had vision, the ability to see an opening where others did not, and he had the courage to pursue that vision.

Gates studied how the world worked. He understood the rules of the game and knew not to waste his energy trying to circumvent the rules.  He was naturally optimistic and had a growth-oriented mindset.  He was extremely intelligent, motivated, and driven.  He dreamed big dreams. He wanted to win, so he prepared himself to win.  He knew he couldn't succeed making his dreams a reality on his own; he needed a team, so he built one.  Gates was in the right place at the right time.  He caught the wave and rode it for all it was worth.  He created and delivered value and by so doing empowered everyone.

Microsoft, the world's largest software company, the business Gates and his partner Paul Allen built, is somewhat analogous to a money system.  Software operates in the virtual domain of digits like money operates in the intangible domain of trust.  Like money, software causes real things to happen; it causes people to take action, to do things. Software, like money, leverages the residual value of labor. The complex code written today rests on the backbone of simpler code crafted yesterday; the contributions of earlier programmers endure.  And like money, software too takes on a life of its own.  People value what the software causes to happen, not the "ones" and "zeros" the "on" and "off" of binary digital reality.

Bill Gates is worth a lot of money because he built Microsoft.  Microsoft is worth a lot of money because of what Microsoft software enables, because of the problems it solves and the actions it facilitates.  The software itself is a compilation of code, symbols controlling a binary "on-off" sequence.  The value in software is the expression of human ideas and actions: labor.  The virtual workings of software translate into actions, which translate into feelings.  From virtually nothing, value is created.  Gates built the largest individual fortune in the world by doing what others couldn't, by advancing when others wouldn't and by creating every step of the way.

## Setting Up for Success

At home Gates' parents encouraged competition in everything from athletics to playing cards to board games. Gates particularly liked Risk and Monopoly. Nearly every household task was made into a contest complete with winners and losers. The winners would get a reward while the losers would endure a penalty. Gates relished striving for excellence.

Like two other notable over-achievers, Thomas Edison and Andrew Carnegie, Gates was a voracious reader. He read everything he could get his hands on. Still today Gates consumes books like most people consume entertainment. He is constantly manipulating ideas in his mind. He looks to make connections, draw conclusions and sift for opportunities.

Early on Gates' parents sensed he might be bored in public school. At age thirteen he enrolled in the Seattle Lakeside School an exclusive preparatory institution. Gates flourished in that prep-school environment, excelling in all his subjects particularly math and science.

In the late 1960's some progressive mothers from the school's Mothers Club used profits from a rummage sale to purchase a teletype terminal and some computer time for students. The computer captivated Gates. He spent much of his free time working on the terminal. He cut his teeth programming by writing a tic-tac-toe program to play against the computer.

Gates met Paul Allen at the Lakeside School. They ended up running the computer lab together. Gates and Allen at one point had their computer privileges revoked for hacking into the computer company's system and procuring free computer time. Once they were allowed computer access again they offered to debug the computer company's system.

Gates and Allen, as high schoolers were developing computer applications in a fledgling industry. When Gates was fifteen he and Allen wrote a computer program to monitor Seattle traffic. They earned a quick $20,000.00 for their efforts. That success set the pair on a path to start a computer business. The boys' parents however, insisted they finish high school first and at least give college a try.

In the fall of 1973, after nearly maxing his SAT, Gates enrolled in Harvard University. While his family expected him to pursue law, Gates focused on the computer lab. The computer was Gates' creative tool; he was only just learning what it could do, the possibilities seemed endless. Allen, after a couple years at Washington State University, dropped out and took a job with a company in Boston, Massachusetts. Allen and Gates were together again.

## Taking a Chance

In the 1970's the computer industry as a whole was still dominated by main frame computer companies and a loose-knit community of hobbyists. The average person didn't have use for a computer. The tide was turning however. Momentum was building and Gates and Allen were poised to ride the wave.

Gates business strategy was one part genius, one part bravado, and one part grit. Gates would focus on finding a programming need to fill. Once he found a need he would promote a solution, a solution he and his team often had not yet developed. Once he had the prospect sold on his solution Gates and his team would get to work; making the bold promise a reality. The end-state for Gates was to match a specific software product with a specific programming need. With the utmost confidence Gates committed his team to doing things that had never been done; and more often than not, they delivered.

The very first opportunity came in 1975 when Gates and Allen saw a need for something to drive a new mini-computer called the Altair 8800. They contacted the manufacturer to see if he was interested in software they were producing to run the machine, software they had not yet written. When the manufacturer asked for a demonstration Gates and Allen got to work. The software they developed ran like a charm and Microsoft was born.

Microsoft was one of many upstart software developers in an industry starting to team with upstart software developers. The personal computing revolution was just beginning. It was like a gold rush, not for virile prospectors, rather for computer geeks. More and more people were beginning to see the potential computers offered. They were beginning to realize what wants and needs the computer might fulfill.

Microsoft pursued a number of prospects, but their big break came by way of Gates' mom. Gates' mother was on the board of the computer giant IBM and IBM was determined to make a splash in the still churning waters of the personal computer market. In late 1980 IBM was searching for software to operate their soon to be released personal computer (PC). Gates convinced IBM's leadership that Microsoft had what they needed, though they did not. Gates, ever resourceful, rushed out and bought an operating system from another developer. He then turned around and licensed that software, MS-DOS, to IBM. As the IBM PC and PC clones began to dominate the personal computer market the MS-DOS operating system gained prominence. Additional maneuvering and a little hardball by Gates eventually ensured Microsoft's dominance.

Gates could have been a protégé of John D. Rockefeller. He saw an opportunity in a fledgling industry and went "all in". He scaled up rapidly, leveraged relationships, and exploited openings to dominate all competitors. Rockefeller controlled nearly 90 percent of the petroleum industry, a monopoly so powerful the government had to break it up. Gates had Microsoft software running on 90 percent of the world's computers. Having such a dominant position in computer software the government nearly broke Microsoft up. In his day Rockefeller was the richest man in the world with a fortune valued in today's terms in the hundreds of billions of dollars. At one point in 1999 Gates holdings in Microsoft were valued at over $100 billion making him the richest man in the world. It seems the faces change but the storyline renews and the cycle continues.

Gates was personally ready to succeed. He played by the rules. He was driven to succeed and gave no quarter to fear. He realized he needed a team so he built a capable team comprised of men and women who were as driven as he was. And he went with the tide. He headed where the opportunities were. He played his part expertly. He created value and made lots of money. So much money he now spends his days giving it away.

## Panning for Gold

- It's good to be born with advantages, but everyone has advantages; success is a matter of developing and exploiting those advantages.
- Vision, drive and the willingness to take risks are distinguishing traits of achievers.
- Competition is most helpful when it improves performance.
- Find partners you respect and trust.
- There is no time like the present to get started.
- Go with the tide; ride the wave.
- Dream big dreams, and then turn those dreams into reality.
- Take calculated risks.
- Build a team, a high-performance team to achieve outstanding results.
- Leverage relationships to exploit opportunities and create value.
- Go for it.

# CHAPTER 10

# HOW LIFE WORKS

**Playing by the rules is the only way to win.**

## Rules of the Game

Everything is in constant motion. We are always moving through time and space. Every life starts somewhere and ends somewhere else. Life is a journey. This journey of life has boundaries; we are constrained by design. We must obey certain laws. In life, as with making money, to succeed we must play by the rules.

So then: How does it all work? How does life work? What are the rules of the game?

Here are the three, not the only, but the three most important rules of the game.

The universe is expanding at an accelerating rate. And for us, from our experience we can determine no matter how extreme the conditions:

**1. Life intends to grow.** Life intends to grow all around us, with us, through us; even despite us, if need be. Life intends to grow.

Next is the rule that if you understand this truth will allow you to realize you are in charge of your journey:

**2. Thoughts become things.** Thought is the mechanism, the power that causes the energy out there everywhere in the universe to form, to coalesce, into the reality we experience. Every thing is first created in mind, in imagination, and then it is created in physical reality. Through thought human beings connect to universal source. Thoughts quite literally become things.

**3. Effort comes before reward.** People receive in proportion to the effort they put forth. We get in proportion to what we give. Money made is the result of value created. Creation comes first.

Remember these:

**Life intends to grow.**

**Thoughts become things.**

**Effort before reward.**

You see, life does not happen to you; life happens through you. Making money, everything we have been exploring, is the process of manipulating energy. Creating is the process of letting energy flow through you. How much energy you manipulate and to what ends determines how much money you make, and how you experience life.

Don't resist these rules; play by the rules and make lots of money.

## The Lens We See Through

See it and then you will believe it. Isn't that the way it typically works?

"I will be wealthy once I have accumulated a great deal of money. Once I see it, then I'll believe it."

Most people wait and watch and hope and pray for the right circumstances to come along and the stars to align to make money. They wait and watch and hope and pray that their tendencies shift, weaknesses disappear, and habits magically change. Usually, mostly, typically nothing spectacular happens. They watch other people grow rich while they sit on the sidelines.

You want to make money. You want to be wealthy. It's time to stop wanting and just be.

We know energy is not distributed equally. And we know everyone starts their journey from a different place, with certain advantages and disadvantages. Making money does not depend on where you are or what happened in the past. What matters is playing by the rules and creating. The greatest challenge we confront is the lens we look through: how we see this world and what we believe.

Each of us approaches life, and approaches making money, from a certain perspective. That perspective is our belief system, our operating paradigm. Our belief system determines the money making habits we cultivate which in turn determine the results we enjoy or endure; what we create.

Every life rests on a foundation of core beliefs. Core beliefs are an individual's most personal and powerful beliefs about this world, themselves, and their place in this world. A positive core belief says, *"The world is a safe, welcoming place. I am capable, connected, and supported. And I have a purpose for being here."* A negative core belief says, *"The world is a dangerous place. I am incapable, disconnected and without support. And I don't have any real purpose for being here."* We craft our core beliefs over a lifetime. Core beliefs color everything we feel, think and do. Core beliefs are the lens through which human beings interpret the world.

Core beliefs dictate whether someone sees a glass half empty or half full; whether they must be ready at a moment's notice to fight or flee; and whether they can actually tap into and release their potential to create. Core beliefs cause people to settle in or push forward. Core beliefs motivate people to make or take money.

The good news is that since we fashion our own core beliefs we can change them. It's just typically not easy. Changing core beliefs is a matter of motivation and employing the discipline of habit.

Every person has the ability to create. Every person has the ability to make money or take money. It's a question of choice. Two motivating forces common to the human experience propel us forward or hold us back: drive and fear.

Drive is the yearning to experience more life; to have more, do more and become more. Drive is that force which ignites desire and pushes us to act. Drive seems to be distributed amongst people in that familiar 80/20 ratio. A few people tend to have the strongest drive.

On the other end of the motivation spectrum is fear. Fear is an expectation of loss: loss of comfort, loss of status, or loss of power. Fear is the great inhibitor of action. Fear holds people back. Fear too seems to be distributed unequally: most people are subject to its influence while few are not.

Drive and fear are two forces influencing how people shape core beliefs. Though we see that drive and fear seem to be innate tendencies we are not condemned to be bound by either. We can change. If we choose to we can go farther, faster; we just have to act. And the most powerful, built-in action management system we human beings possess is our habits process. We can boost our drive, overcome our fears and reshape our core beliefs by routinely taking action.

## Creatures of Habit

If you were to consider your entire day, your actions from waking to falling asleep, you would discover a number of habits. These would be little routines you execute without thinking; activities that don't require making deliberate, conscious choices. You would discover habits of feeling, habits of thinking and communicating, and habits of acting in most areas of your life: personal, professional, and social. Our lives are dominated by habits.

Life moves quickly and a lot is happening; but we have an ingrained strategy to optimize results. Human beings are hard-wired to balance *options and effort* to get what we want. We naturally seek shortcuts to get from "A" to "B" by the most direct and fastest route possible. Given two choices, people usually choose the option that gives the greatest reward for the least effort.

Habits are our natural energy conservation device. Habits help people satisfy desires with minimal effort. Unfortunately, quite often we develop habits which ultimately don't serve our long-term best interests; these habits work against us rather than for us.

Actions take place through a process, a cycle. A drive or circumstance initiates the cycle by presenting a stimulus, a cue. People respond to that cue by feeling a desire. They may or may not employ the faculty of mind; conscious thought. Then they act to change how they feel; to satisfy that desire.

The simplified process looks like this:

**Feeling > Thought > Action > Result**

We encounter or manufacture a stimulus. Something cues us or generates a feeling, a desire, a longing within. Being the rational, considerate beings we believe ourselves to be, we typically thoughtfully consider options and after careful, sensible deliberation we act.

**Not really.** Most often things don't happen this way. **We don't think, we just act.** We move from stimulus, to feeling, immediately to action. Life is primarily a feeling-action-feeling process.

A substantial amount of our time, energy and effort is consumed by habits: pre-determined routines of feeling, thinking, and mostly of acting.

Is that good or bad? Remember habits are a short cut; our means of maximizing reward while minimizing effort.

Habits accomplish the magical result of maximum reward for minimal effort by eliminating thought from the process. A habit sequence looks like this:

**Feeling  >  Action  >  Result  >  Thought**

(Rationalization)

Habits get us from "A" to "B" by the shortest route possible. Thinking is time-consuming and for many painfully difficult, so why waste time and effort thinking? By executing a desire-satisfying routine over and over again; we settle into a process that, with minimal effort, accomplishes the goal of getting the feeling we are after. Through habits we navigate the path of least resistance unconsciously.

We human beings are creatures of habit.

Fortunately the habits process is a tool, a tool we can program; a tool we can control. The habits process is a means to help re-program our core beliefs. By changing our habits we can change the results we achieve. The more we change the results we produce the more our beliefs about how things work will change. Eventually by changing what we believe we influence our core beliefs about the world, ourselves and our place in the world.

People who are not creating all they can create; who are not making all the money they can make, believe to some degree they are separate and alone in a dangerous world. These core beliefs become habits of feeling, thinking and acting. The results habits manifest over time are an expression of who we **believe** ourselves to be. We can change the beliefs by taking new action; by changing our habits. This takes motivation and discipline, but if you are not in the right place, the right state of mind to create, you will not make money. Change your habits and change your life.

Core beliefs are basic programming, an operating paradigm, a person's default approach to life. Core beliefs color how people approach life and how people approach making money. Your core beliefs about this world, yourself and your place in this world are influencing your interpretation of the perspective offered in *Money, The New Science of Making It.* Recognizing that making money is all about empowering and manipulating the flow of energy is a paradigm shift; a shift with significant implications. The most powerful implication however is that if you want to make money, not take money, you can make all you want by creating it.

## Panning for Gold

- Life operates by certain laws; rules of the game. To make money comply with these rules:
  - o   Life Intends to Grow.

- o   Thoughts Become Things.
- o   Effort before Reward.
- Core beliefs are the lens through which people see. Core beliefs influence everything a person does.
- Core beliefs are powerful, personal beliefs a person holds about the nature of this world, her capabilities and connections, and her purpose for being.
- Two personal forces propel or inhibit people's advance: drive and fear.  These forces, though common to everyone, are not equally powerful in everyone.
- Any individual can boost his or her drive and overcome fear.
- Human beings have a built-in energy conservation device known as the "*habits process*".
- Habits are routine actions executed to satisfy specific desires.  Habits take thought out of the equation.
- Typically people feel, then act, then feel.  Life is a feeling-action-feeling process.
- We can use our *habits process* to change beliefs.  By changing what we do results change.  With new results beliefs begin to change.
- Change habits, change lives.

# CHAPTER 11

# CAN'T GO IT ALONE

## Creating is always a collaboration.

### In this Together

Your mother may have told you, "You are here to help others." This begs the question, "What exactly are the others here for then?" Shouldn't they be here for us; to help us?

That is exactly how money works; it's a system to help us. The entire monetary system is a social construct. It gets its power only if and when people are willing to trust each other and trust the system. Money works because it is a useful system for helping people get what they want. Money helps people change how they feel.

Money, the social construct of money, the currency of trust, facilitates energy manipulation. The bigger the system, the more energy flows. The greater the number of people involved in the system, the more wants and needs to meet, the more desires to satisfy; and the more potential energy to create and release. As a population increases opportunities multiply. More people, more chances to create, connect, and give; more chances to receive and more chances to make money.

We are in this together. When it comes to making money, there is no such thing as going it alone. All things, events, encounters and circumstances are helpful. They are opportunities for us to connect, create and give or opportunities to reassess, learn and change course. If all those people sharing our lives don't seem to be helping, if all those people we encounter on the highways and byways, in the hustle and bustle of life seem more of a hindrance than a help, it might be time to consider we are not seeing the big picture or our lens is cloudy.

For someone inclined to cooperate and collaborate, for someone inclined to solve problems and help people get what they want, for someone inclined to make money, it is obvious: we are not alone. These people are connected. However, to someone inclined to compete, inclined to dominate, inclined to win at all costs, inclined to take money, it's not so obvious at all. These people are disconnected. Each inclination is driven by core beliefs. The truth is we are not traveling alone on this road. This is a collective journey. We can't succeed alone and we can't make money alone. We need people and people need us. To make money there is no getting around it, we must help each other.

Many people think life is all about money, when money itself is actually about people. An interesting and at times troubling dynamic of a monetary system is its ability to make life more impersonal. Money serves as an intermediary between people, a medium of exchange. With money and the aid of evolving technology, increasingly people detach from economic transactions. They are distancing themselves from other people. The more we automate the exchange process the greater the distance grows between people, even people trying to serve one another. We tend to forget people are behind all those transactions. It is people's wants and needs we attempt to satisfy. People's trust keeps the system functioning. Though we may not acknowledge this often enough, fundamentally a system of money is all about people relating to people.

Each individual possesses strengths and weaknesses, special gifts and talents. Each individual can create value, can add value, and through a monetary system can exchange value. The system of money is a social system and even though it has its drawbacks it can bring people together. The system can isolate or connect us; it depends on how we use it.

Working together people encourage each other, inspire each other and support each other. Together people are stronger, more intelligent and more capable than they can possibly be alone. We are in this together, like it or not.

## Compete or Collaborate

The discipline of economics is based on the notion of scarcity; managing the distribution of scarce resources. Scarcity is a perspective; a view of the world. It is not the only worldview. Economists observe, on the one hand, the insatiable desires of the human population. On the other hand economists determine there is not enough of practically anything to satisfy all those wants and needs. Therefore economists focus on the efficient allocation and distribution of what appear to be limited resources. Trying to make sense of competing wants and needs, economists tend to operate from a perspective of lack. Is lack, is scarcity the right worldview?

Is there enough air? Is there enough water? Is there enough energy and natural resources to produce food, and clothing, and shelter?

There are enough natural resources. There are enough people with ideas and energy to meet every conceivable want and need. There is more than enough of what we need. The challenge is always control and distribution: two distinctly human functions. Scarcity is always and only a human creation. The problem is not having enough or the capability to create enough, the problem is always a matter of choice. Scarcity is a social problem; a problem of power distribution and management.

This world of ours is a world of contrasts, of opposites. Every state or condition has an opposite. Contrast allows us to experience a given condition. We need *up* to experience *down*, we need *in* to experience *out*, we need *black* to experience *white*, and we need *negative* to experience *positive*; you get the picture. Without contrasts people could not make distinctions. Regarding forces or action: for every action there is an equal and opposite reaction. For every application of force there exists a counterbalancing force. In a monetary system the opposites are to create or destroy; to create money or destroy money; to create value or destroy value. The "value" itself is always a social construct. Value is a product of what people do collectively.

From a consumption or demand standpoint, other people provide what we need. After survival all human wants and needs are social. Even meeting most survival needs requires the cooperative efforts of many people. Security is primarily a social undertaking; as are needs to belong and the drive to attain social status. From a needs hierarchy perspective, virtually everything we desire comes from or by way of other people. We value most what other people do.

From a production or supply standpoint, other people contribute to everything we produce. Infrastructure, machinery, and communication, production and distribution systems provide every resource allowing us to create. All products and services require the collaborative efforts of thousands of people, perhaps hundreds of thousands of people. People contribute to the process in real time or through the enduring residual value of labor. Converting resources from one form to another is manipulating energy.

Manipulating energy for a monetary purpose is never a solitary job. An individual creates and contributes but it is always the energy of the collective that delivers.

Virtually all opportunities in life, and absolutely all opportunities to make money come through, are expressed or manifest by way of other people; no exceptions. In a money system every individual has a decision to make: Compete or collaborate?

People compete from two decidedly different motives. The desire to win or at least compete well athletically, socially, and professionally may raise an individual's, a team's or an organization's performance level. The ultimate outcome may be to generate more value than would have been possible without competing; a positive use of competition. On the other hand, competition often is a struggle for dominance. People take sides and oppose each other, wasting energy and effort pushing against one another rather than pulling together. This kind of competition draws competitors into a state of lack. In this instance competition proves counterproductive; someone loses and quite often everyone loses.

In the midst of heated competition too often humanity is sacrificed for some reward; what is perceived as a scarce resource, a valuable prize to gain. Status, dominion and power are usually the feeling motives behind unconstrained competition. "No holds barred" competition, a struggle where the rules of fair play and sportsmanship are discarded, usually results in destroying value rather than creating value and no one benefits; no one wins.

Money is a social system. It is a system intended to help people. Individuals and groups however, still have a choice to make. We are free to choose not to help. Do we compete or collaborate?

## The Age of Cultivating Relationships

The food production and distribution system in the United States has become so efficient relatively few people actually work in agriculture any more. As a society we have learned to leverage the residual value of labor and the physical resource of energy to feed everyone. We may no longer live in the agricultural age, but to succeed making money we still have to be good at cultivating. Instead of cultivating food, we must cultivate relationships.

To go far and go fast; to have more, do more and become more; to succeed in life and to make money, surround yourself with and routinely associate with positive, growth minded, and supportive people. These are the types of people that create value; the types of people that can make money.

Positive, growth-oriented individuals help other people maintain positive attitudes and growth mindsets. A positive attitude and growth mindset are what an individual requires to synchronize with life. Life intends to grow. People with a positive attitude and growth mindset are actively growing. By maintaining an optimistic state positive people harmonize with creative energy. Positive, growth-oriented people make good things happen and allow good things to happen. They are attuned to opportunities to create value. Positive, growth-oriented people will help you see opportunities and encourage you to take risks. They will help you get out of your comfort zone, where you can try new things and produce new results. Maybe even make some money.

The right support network of people will push you, challenge you, and test you. The right support network of positive, growth-oriented people will help you create more value and will help you make more money. If you don't have a supportive, inspiring network of people surrounding you it is time to establish a network-building, a relationship-building habit. It is time to cultivate relationships.

Making money, the entire system, is a social endeavor. Though by employing money we can convince ourselves the system is impersonal and "business is not personal" don't believe it. Making money is all about people. Making money is all about helping people.

The system, the monetary system, has a demand side, a pull or consumption component and a supply, a push or production component. An economic system, our monetary system is dynamic. It's made up of wants and needs, desires to satisfy, and operates by trust. Every member of society moves back and forth from the consumption to the production side. For someone, for you or me to make money we need relationships on both sides of the economic equation. We need relationships with people to serve, consumers with wants and needs to satisfy. And we need relationships with people who create value; producers, who also have wants and needs to satisfy.

The system serves the collective interest by allowing individuals to pursue their own self-interest. An enlightened perspective is one that realizes the collective interest and the individuals' self-interest are ultimately one and the same.

To make money connect with and relate to people; cultivate relationships. Establish or connect with a community to serve, and build a team with which to create and deliver value.

It's not so much about the number of people you serve or the number you have on your team. It's about the quality of the people you have on your team and what together you can leverage. The relationships themselves are secured by a mutual bond of trust and respect between people.

In an agricultural metaphor, consider creating value as akin to nurturing crops. In the same way one prepares the soil, adds fertilizer, plants seeds, waters and tends to weeds, do the same with relationships. Cultivate relationships and create and deliver value; make money. Make cultivating relationships a habit and you will make money automatically. Connect with and surround yourself with the best people. Making money is all about relationships. Start cultivating yours.

## Panning for Gold

- A monetary system is meant to help people.

- The power in an economy is the social currency of trust. The greater the number of people involved in an economy, the more opportunity and potentially the more power.

- Making money is purely and always a social endeavor. There is no going it alone.

- The intermediary of money allows people to treat business as impersonal.

- Working together people are more capable and powerful than they are working separately.

- The dominant economic worldview is one of scarcity.

- Scarcity is always and only a social construct.

- Believing in scarcity causes "unproductive" competition.
- All opportunities to make money come by way of other people, no exceptions.
- Every individual must decide to compete or collaborate.
- Consumption and production are social components of a social system. People represent both sides of the economic equation: supply and demand.
- To make money cultivate relationships with people to serve and people who produce.
- Success making money is a matter of cultivating productive relationships.

# CHAPTER 12

# SOMETHING BIGGER THAN ME

*To every thing there is a season, and a time to every purpose under heaven.*

## What Goes Around Comes Around

World governments, using the instrument of central banks, have been trying feverishly for years to stave off the negative turns of the business cycle. The powers that be believe that with a little guidance and the right amount of stimulation they can control markets and effectively manage human behavior. Through monetary and fiscal policy they attempt to keep the good times rolling.

Politicians and central bankers are never concerned during growth stages of the business cycle. The sentiment is "pedal to the metal" and "full speed ahead". Politicians and bankers get caught up in the hysteria of good times. They commit an inordinate amount of time to patting themselves on the back for society's good fortune. When the tough times come, as they inevitably do, politicians and central bankers alike focus on finding fault and fixing blame; always on those other guys. Somehow what seemed manageable, what seem doable, what seemed in control, gets out of control. The situation is too big, the circumstances too great for mere mortals to manage. Maybe, just maybe we can't have our cake and eat it to.

The idea of there existing a cycle in economic affairs, what we refer to as the "business cycle", has been around since the early part of the 19<sup>th</sup> century. The business cycle is the notion that an economy expands and contracts, grows and shrinks in cycles. The more analysts were able to compile and quantify economic data the more evident business cycles, periods of economic expansion followed by economic contraction, became. The reasons for these cycles were, and from an economic standpoint remain, unclear.

The business cycle is typically monitored today by measuring fluctuations in real gross domestic product (GDP). These fluctuations in economic activity range from slow to moderate to rapid expansion (booms), to periods of stagnation, contraction, and accelerating decline (busts). While politicians and central bankers attempt to moderate downturns, the cycle persists.

The business cycle consists of four phases: expansion / growth, boom / peak, contraction / downturn, and bust / trough. Specific measures define the phases of expansion and contraction. The cycle alternates between periods of positive economic growth and declining economic activity. We label a slowdown of a certain severity and length a recession or depression. After a period of weakening and possibly malaise a recovery begins. As growth accelerates a recovery gains momentum and builds to a boom. A boom inevitably falters and growth stops. Economic activity declines and the cycle begins again.

We don't know exactly what causes a business cycle. Economists have offered a myriad of theories that all boil down to what people do. The business cycle is a social phenomenon. It's bigger than any individual or any specific group of people. The business cycle fluctuates as the tempo of human activity fluctuates. Business cycles are bigger than us.

## Energy Ebbs and Flows

Cycles are an aspect of the social world just as they are a feature of the natural world. The earth spins on its axis causing a recurring cycle of day and night. The moon orbits the earth and exerts gravitational forces we measure in surging and receding tides. The earth revolving around the sun drives a variety of powerful cycles. The rays of the sun deliver energy constantly impacting earth's atmosphere. Water flows in a cycle from ocean to air to ocean again. Life conforms to the rhythm of natural cycles like economies follow the cadence of social cycles.

We are all familiar with seasons: spring, summer, fall and winter. Each season has its own signature, its own feel: the blooming of spring, the heat of summer, the brisk of fall, and the cold and dark of winter. Each of the four seasons compliments the others; each is a necessary part of the cycle. Life adapts to the cycle of seasons.

In this scientific age we tend to think of our lives and history as unfolding in a straight line. We seem to be forever moving forward. But the ancients didn't look at time like we do. To them life wasn't a straight line, it was a cycle. Human lives too pass through phases much like seasons. People move from childhood, to young adult, to middle age, to those elder years. The energy of life ebbs and flows, it surges ahead, speeding up, then throttles back and slows down.

To every thing there is a season.

We recognize seasons in economic activity, the business cycle, but social seasons occur on an even grander scale. William Strauss a historian and Neil Howe an economist have written extensively on the phenomenon and characteristics of generational social cycles.

Like with seasons of the year, we all recognize "generations"; you know, the Baby Boomers. Baby Boomers are the generation born from the early 1940's till the early 1960's. After the Baby Boomers came Generation X. Next came the Millennial generation. These are the young people born from roughly 1980 to the turn of the millennium. And the generation being born now, some call the "Digi" or digital generation. What about the generation before the boomers; our elders today? They are known as the Silent Generation.

Each generation has a unique signature, a unique persona, and like nature's seasons, a unique role to play. A full turn of generational seasons takes approximately eighty years; roughly the length of a human lifespan. The energy of society ebbs and flows through four seasons in about eighty years.

The first season in a generational cycle, spring, is the high; a period of growth and expansion. Society shakes off the cold and dark of winter and begins to surge forward, people pull together. The next season in the generational cycle, summer, is a period of awakening and opportunity. All that energy of spring matures. People, relying on the foundation of social cohesion built in the spring, begin to broaden their focus. Society advances as people diversify, pursuing unique and promising opportunities.

An advance requires the concerted effort of society; a surge of energy. But like with all surges the energy of advance gets spent. The advance reaches its apex and then energy begins to wane. The slowing ushers in the season of fall, a period of unraveling. Having pulled together in the spring and awakened to individual opportunities in the summer, people turn to a new agenda. An attitude of "every man for himself" prevails. Competition increases and as a result the community fractures. Cool breezes blow as the warmth of summer dissipates and a cold, dark season arrives.

The final season of the generational cycle, winter, is the season of discontent; the season of divisiveness, suspicion and struggle. Winter is the social season of crisis.

We can trace this seasonal pattern of generations back hundreds, even thousands of years. The United States is now on its fourth seasonal cycle. The first generational cycle ended with the American Revolution. The second ended eighty years later with the American Civil War. The third ended, eighty years after that, with World War II. This brings us to, now: 2015. We are in the midst of the winter season; the season of crisis.

Each season in a generational cycle serves a purpose: spring, the high; summer, the awakening; fall, the unraveling; and winter, the crisis. The high is a time of pulling together, of civic virtue and renewal. The awakening is a rejection of the conformity of the high; people begin to open themselves to other opportunities. They search for truth and while the times are good, they make their own way. During the unraveling individuals drift farther apart and the tide turns. During the fall people stop pulling together, the collective energy recedes and then winter settles in.

Winter is the period of crisis; the era of creative destruction. "Every man for himself" has gone too far. The collective energy of the people is spent. Winter is a time of conflict and soul-searching and ultimately recuperation. Individuals must choose to risk it all to reassert the civic virtue of a high; to change direction and bring about the renewal of spring. If the society fails to come together the prospects for progress turn grim and winter persists.

These generational seasons are natural and necessary cycles of life. Energy ebbs and flows, surges and recedes like tides across humanity.

Each generation has its own persona, its own signature, its own style and its own role to play. Strauss and Howe have demonstrated the generations always recur in the same order and exhibit the same archetypal tendencies: *Artists*, *Prophets*, *Nomads* and *Heroes*.

The Silent Generation, our elders now, are *Artists*. They were born in a winter season, the season of crisis, the Great Depression and World War II. The Silent Generation of artists came of age in good times; the period of social cohesion and economic expansion following World War II.

Baby Boomers are *Prophets*, idealists, set on changing the world. Baby Boomers were born in the season of spring, the high. They came of age to fuel the awakening, that era of sex, drugs and rock-n-roll; the 1960's and 1970's.

Generation X, born in the 1960s and 1970s of that awakening are *Nomads*. The nomads are a generation of youngsters left to fend for themselves. In the case of Generation X, these are the latchkey kids. Left to their own devices, as older generations were preoccupied, members of Generation X grew up to be practical, pragmatic and independent; some might say, jaded and cynical.

The Millennials represent America's new generation of *Heroes*. This is the generation, like the GI generation that won World War II, meant to pull together and save our world. Destiny however, is not pre-ordained. How winter evolves; the challenges society faces and the course individuals choose to pursue; will determine how the crisis unfolds and whether the heroes will have an opportunity to live up to their billing.

The generation being born now, the digital generation, born in the crisis, in the winter season is the next generation of *Artists*. The cycle renews.

Each generation has a specific role to play in the turning of the seasons. Each generation balances the strengths and weaknesses of the others as spring turns to summer turns to fall turns to winter. We are in the winter season; the crisis era. How the generations pull together; how the generations rise to fulfill their roles will quite literally determine the fate of this nation and the fate of our world.

You and I are each members of a generation; we have roles to play. Social cycles are massive. They drive changes individuals must adapt to. We are in the winter season, the crisis era. We may not be able to change the weather, but we can deal with the season which is upon us. Pulling together we can endure the cold and dark; together we can emerge into the warmth and light of spring.

## We is Bigger than Me

Forces operate in the natural world; forces much more powerful than you and me; than human beings. Forces operate in the social world; forces much more powerful than you and me; than individuals. Forces operate in the economic world, in trade and commerce, in the world of making money; forces more powerful than you and me. We must adapt.

We live at the mercy of cycles. We can't change the seasons and we can't control the tides. Trying is a waste of time, energy and effort. We collectively rise when the tide surges and we collectively sink when the tide recedes. Cycles, natural and social and economic, are a fact of life. The best we can do is recognize which season we are in and which way the tide is flowing. Then we can prepare ourselves appropriately. We can do the best we can with what we've got.

Making money is only and always a social undertaking. No one makes money alone. Money represents trust, a social bond, person to person. Making money is the process of adding value; of helping other people get what they want; of helping other people change how they feel. Making money is a social process. Don't try to go it alone. We are all in this together.

Life operates by certain rules. Making money operates by certain rules. Knowing how to play the game is an important part of knowing how to make money. Money is made by creating and delivering value. We create value when we manipulate energy to positive ends. Prepare yourself to make money by getting your core beliefs straight. You deserve to be wealthy. Get your habits process working for you. Step by step, habit by habit advance.

Scarcity is a social construct with no basis in the natural world. Resources are not scarce. Opportunities are not scarce. Wants and needs are unlimited. There is no shortage of people to help. Energy is always flowing. Don't resist the tide, go with it and create. Cultivate relationships and you cultivate opportunities. There are forces bigger than you and me and we must be aware of those forces. But together we can do anything. *We* is bigger than *me*. So as you consider the nature of things remember, making money is all about *we*, not about *me*. Get yourself right then join the party and create. You will then earn your keep.

## Panning for Gold

- Politicians and central bankers cannot control human behavior.

- The "business cycle" is a social cycle representing the energy flow in economic activity.

- The business cycle has four phases: expansion, boom, contraction, and bust.

- Cycles are an aspect of the natural and social world.

- Energy ebbs and flows through human generations.

- A generational cycle lasts approximately 80 years.

- A generational cycle moves through four phases: a high (pulling together), an awakening (drifting apart), an unraveling (division and conflict) and a crisis (creative destruction pointing toward renewal).

- Each generation has a role to play in social cycles.

- We are in the winter season, the crisis era.

- Cycles and seasons are bigger than individuals.

- The best anyone can do is recognize the season and prepare accordingly.

- Making money, creating value, is about pulling together. We are in the crisis era, the time of greatest risk, and greatest opportunity. It is time to pull together.

# PART 4

## ALCHEMY

## ALL THAT GLITTERS ISN'T GOLD

Making money is a process, a scientific process. People make money by doing things a certain way; by creating and contributing; by adding value to the energy flow. Money represents the energy of people. Where people direct their focus energy flows. Money flows where attention goes. Everyone has what they need to create and contribute; to make money. Making money is a matter of doing something; of opening the floodgates and letting energy flow.

# CHAPTER 13

## THAT'S ENTERTAINMENT

**When they laugh, when they cry, when they rejoice, when they let go of their worries; that's entertainment.**

### Destiny or Drive?

Beyoncé Knowles, a 33 year-old singer, songwriter and actress was the highest paid performer in 2014, she earned $115 million. Her net worth is approaching half a billion dollars. She went from obscurity to fame and fortune; from winning a school talent contest at the age of seven to one of the most recognizable, admired, and powerful celebrities in the world in less than sixteen years. How is it possible that so much energy flowed her way?

Beyoncé was born and grew up in Houston, Texas. Her mother was a hairdresser, her father a Xerox sales manager. She had a natural talent for singing and by age eight was part of a six-girl group called Girl's Tyme playing the Houston talent show circuit. Girl's Tyme was good enough to compete on *Star Search* a nationally televised talent show. By age ten Beyoncé was enrolled in a music magnet school. From the start she directed her energy toward her strength: performing. She intended to do the best she could with what she had.

Girl's Tyme, trimmed back to a four-girl group, signed with Columbia records in 1995. In 1996 Girl's Tyme, renamed Destiny's Child released a critically acclaimed single. They followed with a song for the soundtrack to the hit movie *Men in Black*, and in 1998 released their debut album. Destiny's Child shot to the top of the pop charts and never looked back. The group earned critical acclaim and entertained audiences around the world until disbanding in 2005. Beyoncé, while committed to Destiny's Child, worked hard and pursued other opportunities as her star began to rise.

In 2001 Beyoncé landed her first of many acting roles in a made for television musical *Carmen*. In 2003 while on hiatus from Destiny's Child Beyoncé released her debut solo album. That album sold 11 million copies, earned Beyoncé five Grammy Awards and established her as a solo artist on the world stage. The more she shared her talent, the more people responded and directed their attention toward her. As people's attention focused on Beyoncé money flowed her way.

## An Iron Man

Robert Downey, Jr., a supremely talented, former alcoholic and drug abuser, was the highest grossing actor of 2014. He earned $75 million dollars pretending; playing men he was not, in a fantastical world. Acting Downey showed aspects of his true self, as all great performers must, and genius shined through.

Robert Downey Jr. has proved himself to be an iron man enduring and overcoming the demons he faced. His fortune was made despite years of pain, heartache and struggle. His vocation is connecting with people to help them feel a range of emotions, from joy to sorrow and from terror to relief. Downey captures the imaginations of men and women around the world. Touching people's hearts through his art he offers them an opportunity to feel. Allowing others to change how they feel he entertains and draws attention to himself.

Downey was born into a family of performers. His father was an actor and film maker, his mother an actress. He grew up with an older sister in Greenwich Village on the island of Manhattan in New York City. Downey's father was a drug addict. Downey took his first hit of marijuana at age six. He recalls abusing drugs and alcohol as a child as bonding experiences with his father. He had some high hurdles to overcome. Young Downey was not afraid of failure however; rather he was afraid of mediocrity. He determined to pursue his dream of becoming an actor with gusto; failure was not an option.

Downey, like Beyoncé, took naturally to performing; he made his acting debut in 1970 at the age of five in one of his father's films. He studied the performing arts: dance, music, and acting through his elementary and high school years. After his parents divorced Downey moved with his father to California. In 1982 he dropped out of high school and headed back to New York to pursue acting fulltime and began to build a resume in off-Broadway theater roles. In 1985 he was cast as part of a new young troop of performers for *Saturday Night Live*. When ratings failed to improve however, he was replaced. 1985 proved to be Downey's breakthrough year. He secured supporting roles in big-screen movies and by 1987 had his first leading role.

The 1990's was a whirl-wind decade for Downey. He continued to struggle with drugs and alcohol even while he devoted himself to his craft of acting. He starred in a string of critically acclaimed and publicly well-received movies.

121

He was nominated for an Academy Award for his starring role as Charlie Chaplin in 1992. He married that same year and had a son in 1993. As his acting career took off his love affair with drugs and alcohol blossomed careening his personal life and career down a desperate path.

Downey had his first run-in with the law in 1996 and things went from bad to worse. He continued to abuse drugs, was arrested, and served multiple stints in jail and at court ordered substance abuse centers. After five years of abuse, rehab and relapse Downey turned a corner and realized he could not overcome his addition on his own; he asked for help. By 2003 he began his comeback in earnest. With the help of friends and by employing the same focus and determination he exhibited as a young man to never settle for mediocrity, he went back to work.

Downey's big financial break came when he was cast as the Marvel comic book character Iron Man, in a movie by the same name released in 2008. Since then Downey as starred in six movies grossing more than $500 million worldwide: three Iron Man movies, *The Avengers*, and two Sherlock Holmes adventures. Downey has soared to the top of his field.

More than anything people want to feel. Men and women, who through their art, help people to feel excited, powerful, loving and joyful, get people's attention, and where attention goes money flows.

## Among the Very Best

Floyd Mayweather, Jr. pound-for-pound one of the best boxers, if not the best, in the history of the sport, earned $105 million in 2014. Mayweather was the highest paid athlete that year. At an age when most boxers are past their prime Mayweather continues to school elite boxers from across the globe about what it means to be a world champion. Like Robert Downey, Jr. Mayweather grew up surrounded by drugs and alcohol, but to make matters worse his was a world of poverty and violence. Mayweather had talent, he had skills, but, as he put it, 'No one knows the hell he had to endure.' It seems his life story could have been a footnote in the annals of history but instead he continues to captivate the world; attention and money flow to him.

Born to a boxing family Mayweather never seriously considered any other career choice. His grandmother saw his potential and encouraged him. When Mayweather suggested it was time for him to get a real job, his grandmother told him, 'Just keep boxing.' Her advice paid off handsomely.

Mayweather's mother was an addict, his father, once a welterweight contender, was a drug dealer who often found himself behind bars. Mayweather's childhood was spent shuttling back and forth between his father's place in Grand Rapids, Michigan and his mother's and grandmother's homes in New Jersey. Mayweather saw, in boxing, an opportunity to take care of his mother so he dropped out of high school to pursue boxing fulltime. He poured everything he had into his martial art.

At the age of 16 in 1993 Mayweather won his first Golden Gloves championship in the 106-pound weight class. The next year he won in the 114-pound weight class, and two years after that he won the Golden Gloves championship in the 125-pound weight class. In the 1996 Atlanta Olympic Games Mayweather won the bronze medal in the featherweight division, losing a controversial decision to a Bulgarian boxer. As an amateur he had an overall 84–6 record.

After the Olympics in 1996 Mayweather turned pro. Boxing commentators immediately recognized Mayweather as a prodigy; one of the best the sport had ever seen. By 1998 he was ranked pound-for-pound eighth in the world. By the next year he ranked pound-for-pound as the second best boxer in the world.

Mayweather's shining moment came when he beat Oscar dela Hoya to win the junior middleweight championship of the world in 2007. That fight brought in a record $120 million on pay-per-view and earned Mayweather a $25 million payday. Since that fight Mayweather retired from boxing and then made a comeback, retired again and the returned to the ring once again. Each time Mayweather's opponents fell his payday's increased.

At the time of this writing Mayweather maintains a professional boxing record of 47–0. He is a five-division world champion, having won ten world titles and championships in four different weight divisions.

While the sport of boxing may not be enjoying the popularity it once did, people around the world still clamor to see the best pugilists in action. Mayweather as perhaps the best that has ever been still gets people's attention and where attention goes, energy flows.


People have only time and opportunity; opportunity to feel. Artists and athletes get people's attention. Through their craft they help people change how they feel. People recognize and admire the skills and abilities and the qualities and characteristics entertainers express. They like how entertainers make them feel, and they long to be what the entertainer's professional persona represents. People aspire to be like celebrities: beautiful, confident, capable and powerful.

Whether the entertainer is a singer or musician, a writer, producer or actor, or a sports hero people see the best in them; they see someone who has it all. Entertainers gain the attention of billions of people around the world by distracting the masses from their ordinary lives, at least for a short while, and allowing them to feel something good. People connect with the energy and emotion artists and competitors embody and share. Entertainers command people's attention. And wherever people direct their attention they direct their energy, and that's entertainment. Where attention goes, money flows.

## Panning for Gold

- Focus on strengths; what you love to do and do best.

- Keep embracing new opportunities.

- Put your heart into what you do. Share your talent, your joy, your love.

- Help people genuinely feel.

- Keep going, despite challenges; never give up.

- Get people's attention and go with the flow.

- People have nothing but time and opportunity to feel.

- People's attention is drawn to flowing energy.

- People idolize men and women who help them feel.

- Where attention goes, money flows.

# CHAPTER 14

# SOMETHING FROM NOTHING

### "Something for nothing"; life just doesn't work that way.

## Something Extraordinary

Alchemy, the mysterious forerunner of modern chemistry, flourished in the Middle Ages. Drawing upon such diverse practices as philosophy, mysticism, sorcery, mythology, and religion adherents attempted to produce magical instruments, powerful elixirs and precious objects. Alchemists are most commonly known for trying to convert base metals into gold and silver. As far as we know, no one succeeded. Alchemy however, is what we practice today when we make money. Making money is the scientific process of transforming something ordinary into something truly extraordinary.

As we dig deeper into the science of making money, it's time to reinforce a couple of points. First, though it is possible to make a case that life is substantially about money, you know in your heart that it is not all about money. Life is much more then economic transactions and it's much broader and deeper than this physical reality of time and space. You can't put a price on the beauty of a sunrise or the embrace of a lover. Some things just cannot be measured or quantified. The second related point is that not all things can be monetized. As some things cannot be converted to a monetary value, people do not accord a monetary value to all things. People are not willing to trade or give up any and everything and they are certainly not willing to buy or pay for any and everything. It is easier to determine in aggregate what people value; things related to satisfying desires; than it is to determine what individuals' value specifically. One person's trash is another person's treasure. It's all so simple in theory, but it can be quite mystifying in practice.

People generally like the idea of getting something for nothing. But, as we know life just doesn't work that way. The source and substance of everything is energy. And though we don't really understand what energy is, we know that energy is not created or destroyed, it just constantly changes form. The process of economic exchange, production, distribution, trade, and consumption, is a process of energy conversion. Something doesn't come from nothing. Something, economic benefit, comes from what people think and do: their ideas and action.

The beauty of science is that if you set the same conditions and introduce the same energy in the same way, you get the same result. Science is about doing things a certain way. The science of making money is about doing things a certain way so as to control a stream of energy: energy which can be monetized.

Unlike the "hard sciences" where practitioners deal almost exclusively with physical substances, the science of making money is primarily social. With a social science it is decidedly more difficult to control for variables to guarantee results. The key with a social science, as with a "hard science", is acting in accordance with natural law; the way life works. By doing things a certain way, results are guaranteed.

Money, a means to change the way people feel, is the currency of trust. An economic system starts and ends with people's desires, their wants and needs. People trust in one another and the system to deliver value; to deliver what they desire, where and when they want it. It really is an amazing system. Money moves from person to person as feelings change. The energy of the economic system flows from person to person as people produce, connect, trade, and consume. People's wants and needs energize the economy and money, like oil in an engine, keeps the whole enterprise moving. Money facilitates the energy flow.

The system, the process, the global economy is already in motion. Trillions of dollars of value flows around the world on a daily basis. Every individual can contribute to the system, to the process; every individual can create and add value. No one has to create something from nothing. Anyone seeking to make money need only understand and focus on a few things.

## Lots of Gray Area

Life is a feeling-action-feeling endeavor. Desires, wants and needs, drive the train. Humans act to convert feelings. Everyone acts to change how they feel in the moment. Some are motivated by longer time lines, some are motivated by shorter, but all people are stirred to act to accomplish the same objective: change how they feel. The economy, a system of economic exchange, is a means to help people get what they want. Focusing on helping people get what they want is what making money is all about.

Making money, creating and adding value, is not the only way to acquire money. People give to one another all the time. We receive what we need when we need it; that's how life works. And of course people can take it. Instead of contributing value people can deliberately withdraw value from the endless stream of energy. How much individuals take influences the flow of energy and the strength of people's trust. Too many people taking too much undermines the entire system.

It is not always easy to distinguish making from taking. If, as I have characterized it, making is on one end of a spectrum and taking is on the other, there exist many shades of gray in between. Individuals' motives and methods are not always clear. If you are interested in making money, adding value, it's not worth devoting time to judging, condemning or blaming other people. What's done is done. A more productive use of time is building a system to promote creation and discourage corruption; a system to help people do the right thing automatically.

A human being is both a consumer and a producer. Every person contributes, creates and produces value and every person withdraws and consumes value. People who make money by creating and adding value become wealthy and prosperous; they approach life differently from the rest. Prosperous people are men and women who earn their money by creating and delivering value.

Nature abhors a vacuum; whatever a person contributes or gives away is immediately replaced. The prosperous engage more frequently and more enthusiastically in the process of creating and giving. By giving they open up space to receive. By creating and giving they accelerate and empower the flow of energy.

While we all make and take money, prosperous people are **net makers** of money.

While we all are at times creditors and debtors prosperous people are **net creditors**.

While we all produce and consume, prosperous people are **net producers**.

While we all give and take, prosperous people are **net givers**.

While we all contribute and withdraw, prosperous people are **net contributors**.

Prosperous people, on average give more than they take and produce more than they consume. Their stores are replenished automatically by infinite, endless supply. Prosperous men and women earn people's trust. Once the current of trust flows toward them they are able to direct the energy flow and amass wealth.

Anyone can do what the prosperous do. Anyone can make money. Follow the science of making money. Do things a certain way and reap the rewards. Build trust.

Changing one's ratio of giving and taking, producing and consuming is not necessarily an easy task. Each person operates from the foundation of core beliefs and each person has built an entire system of personal habits to keep life progressing steadily and predictably. If one's production to consumption ratio is skewed toward consumption, that person is clinging to what they have instead of letting energy flow. That individual must deliberately change course. Changing course is a matter of changing habits. The challenge with habits however, is that it is often easier, more convenient and simpler to settle back into old routines.

Think of "production and consumption" like "diet and exercise". Exercise is putting out effort; producing and giving. Consumption is fueling our bodies to meet our needs so we can act. To maintain health we must be mindful that it is easy to "out-eat" exercise. It is easy, simple and pleasurable, in the short term, to focus on consuming and eat too much. We undermine health and fitness when we eat too much and when we eat the wrong things. As with health, we will never make money if we consume more than we produce. Money represents delivering value. To make money, give more than you take. Create more than you consume and the energy of the universe will flow in your direction.

## Scientific Money Making Process

The process of making money is the process of contributing to the currency of trust by directing energy enlivening the world. Having money means controlling a certain amount of that currency; controlling a certain amount of energy. The more energy one controls the more power and freedom that person has. The more energy you control the more influence you have; the more of everything you can have, the more you can do, and the more you can become.

**A person doesn't need money to control energy, but money, our economic system is the primary means we human beings use to navigate life in our material world. It's not about the money; it's fundamentally about the energy of life.**

Your financial condition; whether you reliably have money or you consistently are in debt is a reflection of your approach to life. Your financial situation is a reflection of you.

What does your "give and take ratio" your "production to consumption ratio" look like? Are you positive and growth oriented? Do you look for opportunities to create and add value? Or are you negative and set in your ways? Do you intend to do just what you need to do to get by? Do you prefer to take what you can?

Money is energy.  How much energy is flowing through your hands?  How much energy is flowing through your life?

If there isn't much energy in your life, you aren't following the scientific process for making money.  For some people making money comes naturally.  They have the disposition, the core beliefs and the drive to look for opportunities and create and deliver value.  Think of the Rothschild's, Rockefeller, and Gates or Beyoncé, Downey, and Mayweather; these people automatically, deliberately and energetically executed the scientific money making process.  For most people however, making money does not come naturally.  For these people, core beliefs are limiting and drive is lacking.  Anyone however, can change.  It becomes a matter of learning and following the scientific money making process.

Every change is a choice; a choice made in a moment.  That choice is to move in a new direction, to do something different.  Moving in a new direction, doing something different ushers in change.  Change is automatic.  Doing things a certain way produces certain results; it's science; it's the law.  Any and every one can follow the money making process and change their lives.

## Scientific Money Making Process

1.  **Transform Self** (feel and think; move in the right direction)
2.  **Find Wants and Needs to Satisfy** (think; find people to help)
3.  **Create** (do; add value; help people)
4.  **Deliver Value** (do; contribute; monetize effort)

Making money is not something you do so as to get back to living life; though most people tend to view "work" this way. Making money is actively contributing to life. The difference between the economic and the personal realm is that in the economic realm output and production are quantified and measured, and money is exchanged. In the personal realm energy is exchanged, it's just not monetized.

The energy of the money-go-round is not separate and distinct from real life; it is very much part of real life. To play in the money making arena, to make money: play by the rules. Employ the process; do things a certain way and energy will flow automatically.

## Panning for Gold

- Making money is the process of transforming something ordinary into something extraordinary.

- Life is not all about the money. Life is about feeling, experiencing, and being.

- Not everything can be monetized.

- Economic exchange is a process of energy conversion.

- Economic benefit is derived from ideas and action.

- Doing things a certain way produces a certain result.

- Wants and needs energize the economic system.

- Money changes from potential energy to kinetic energy as it moves from person to person; as feelings change.

- Trillions of dollars are on the move around the world.

- All people are producers and consumers.

- People who amass wealth consistently produce more than they consume.

- Anyone can make money by doing things a certain way.

- Money represents energy. Having money means having control of energy.

- Scientific Money Making Process:

  Self > Identify Need > Create > Deliver

- Making money is one way of contributing to life's energy flow.

# CHAPTER 15

# ENERGY FLOWS

# WHERE ATTENTION GOES

**Round and round it goes and where it stops nobody knows.**

## Who You Are Matters Most

Do the best you can with what you've got. That's all you can do; and quite frankly that's enough. If the circumstances of your life are not to your liking; if you would like to make more money you must do something different with what you've got. Doing something different produces a different result. Follow the making money process. Start with yourself.

Begin by assessing your core beliefs about this world (safe or dangerous), yourself (connected and capable or alone and lacking), and your place in this world (purposeful or adrift without a purpose). Next consider: Are you inclined to make or take money?

Is your main focus *Experience / Fulfillment* (make) or *Status / Power* (take)?

Is you mindset *Growth Oriented* (make) or *Fixed / Set* (take)?

How do you view challenges, as *Opportunities* (make) or *Obstacles* (take)?

Do your principles guide you to *Play by the Rules* (make) or invoke *Survival of the Fittest* (take)?

Do you look to *Collaborate* (make) or *Compete* (take) with other people?

Is your focus on *What You can Get / Selfish* (take) or *What You Can Give / Selfless* (make)?

To get what you want do you *Create* (make) or *Intimidate, Deceive or Coerce* (take)?

Get a sense of your own tendencies. External circumstances reflect an internal reality. First, to change circumstances change your self. Next consider: making money is about creating and contributing. Are you inclined to create and contribute?

You are likely familiar with a "normal distribution". A normal distribution is a graphical representation of statistical data where occurrences or data points tend to a concentrate around a central value. People's height, weight, age and intelligence, these types of characteristics, tend to occur in a normal distribution around a mean or average value.

## NORMAL DISTRIBUTION

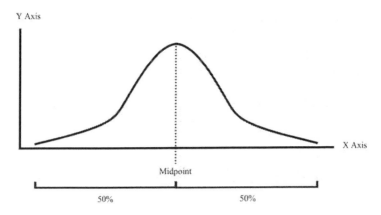

138

Individuals demonstrate unique strengths and weaknesses but human beings are more alike than different. Everyone possesses skills and talents. Everyone has the ability to manipulate energy. Everyone has the ability to create and add value. Most every trait or attribute assessed across the human population plots out as or near a normal distribution. Why then is wealth so skewed? Why is money concentrated in so few hands? If talents and ability are nearly uniformly spread throughout a population why is wealth so concentrated?

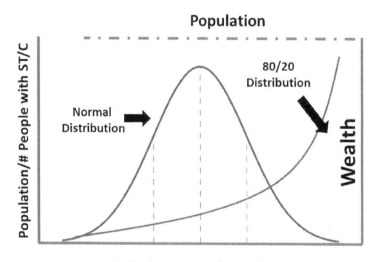

**Skills & Talents / Capabilities**

The answer to the question: "Why is wealth so concentrated?" is simple. Because we make it so; it's a collective decision; not a conscious decision, rather an unconscious one; it's how we make the system work. This simple answer however, is not very helpful.

Let's examine the disparity between the lowest wage earners in America and the highest. The minimum wage in the United States is $7.25 per hour (over half of the states have established a higher minimum wage than the federal standard). At minimum wage a worker grosses $290.00 for a forty-hour workweek. Working fifty-two weeks, a minimum wage worker earns $15,080.00 per year. You probably know people who work for minimum wage. If you are in a public place, you can likely see some just by glancing around. More than a million and half Americans work for minimum wage. On the other hand, more than thirty thousand Americans bring in more than $2,000,000.00 per year.

On average the highest earners are men and women in medical professions, however corporate executives do comparatively well. The average salary for corporate executives in the United States is about $178,000.00 per year. The average Fortune 500 CEO brings home a little more than $10,000,000.00 per year. The average corporate executive makes twelve times what a minimum wage worker earns, while the CEO's of America's largest companies take home 683 times as much as minimum wage workers.

Is this disparity a matter of attributes, traits and characteristics? Are high earners that much more intelligent, educated, creative, insightful, innovative, energetic, committed, and driven, in short capable, than low wage earners? Do they work twelve to hundreds of times harder? Not likely. Something else is happening to concentrate all that money and wealth.

The difference between the minimum wage earner and the average CEO is a factor of the number of desires each has a part in satisfying. It's not how hard they work; it is how many people they serve and how many desires they satisfy. The typical minimum wage earner does not serve as many people or satisfy as many desires as a man or a woman running a business organization serves or satisfies. Energy flows person to person, desire by desire; more energy = more money.

## Working the Levers

Archimedes famously said, 'Give me a lever large enough and a place to stand and I can move the world.' The difference between high earners and low earners, between people who create and monetize lots of value and those who do not, begins with who they are and where they are headed (core beliefs, vision and drive). Beyond that, it's not that high earners are hundreds of times more capable, it's that high earners employ leverage. They work the levers to exploit a mechanical advantage; really a social advantage. High earners, people who control big streams of money, work the levers of trust.

Anyone and everyone can apply leverage through "lever assets":

## Lever Assets

- **Thought:**  the most powerful personal lever a human being controls. Thought is the means to access the universal, limitless *source*. Thought is how people receive and shape the energy of ideas and direct that energy into the world. *Nothing is as powerful as an idea whose time has come.* Ideas ultimately manifest as action. The power and influence of an idea dictates its leverage.

- **Personal Relationships:**  trust built person to person over time with family members, friends, colleagues, customers and acquaintances. A track record of being reliable and getting things done serves as a powerful lever.

- **Other People:**  organizing, motivating and empowering people toward the same end is the most powerful lever of all.  By working together individuals concentrate and multiply the power of thought energy.

- **Residual Value of Labor / Things:**  natural resources, property and capital equipment.  Physical energy (oil, gas, electricity, etc.), machines and technology are sources of concentrated power; potential energy.  The aid of machines and the energy used to power those machines multiplies the effort applied to a task.  Any useful tool represents the sum total of ideas and work applied to create it.  The residual value of labor in a thing is concentrated potential energy.

- **Time:**  Promising a future benefit, delivery of a product or service in the future, or promising a future payment is leveraging trust.

Both sides of the "supply-demand" "production-consumption" equation offer opportunities for leverage.  On the demand / consumption side, the amount of energy involved is a function of the quantity and relative strength of wants and needs to satisfy.  On the supply / production side of the equation, how much energy is involved is a function of leverage.  One person can only physically do so much, can only give so much, can only create so much, but with a big enough lever one person can move the world.

It is possible to acquire money in a variety of ways; these ways boil down to: be given or inherit it; win it; take it; or make it.  Making money is always a matter of doing something; of channeling energy.  To make money an individual might:

- Trade time and energy for a wage (most popular method)

- Exploit a unique skill, talent or expertise as an artist, performer or freelancer

- Sell ideas (information, inventions)

- Invest money in other people's enterprises (leverage money)

- Build a business (leverage both sides of supply–demand equation)

The most common means of making money is by being a "cog" in someone else's machine. Most people settle for the simplest and easiest option, they trade time for a wage as an employee.

Making lots of money however, requires leverage. Many people recognize and pursue growth opportunities with an organization and commit themselves to someone else's idea and system. Other people prefer independence. Possessing an in-demand skill, talent or expertise these people collaborate to create and deliver value while still remaining autonomous. Controlling money to invest allows the investor to exploit time and take advantage of the energy generated through the investment. Far and away however, the greatest opportunity for gaining leverage and making money is through building a business.

Business builders construct levers. The process of building a business is squarely in the energy flow of an economy. An efficient business focuses on meeting wants and needs to the greatest degree possible while also providing an opportunity for producers to produce. A business owner has the opportunity to draw energy from and for production, as well as conduct the value delivery and monetization process of meeting wants and needs. A business builder creates a lever by combining other people's energy flows into his or her system to create and deliver even more value.

## Hit the Sweet Spot

Businesses are built to satisfy desires. Usually, mostly, typically businesses focus on meeting demands that already exist: what people have proven they will pay for. Quite frequently however, opportunities arise to define new desires, to create new demand. People are always looking to change how they feel; sometimes they can be influenced to desire something new. Working in a new area or to meet a unique or newly emerging demand is the realm of the entrepreneur.

We discussed the hierarchy of needs in an earlier section. Simply, economic wants and needs, economic desires, fall into one of three categories:

1. Subsistence needs (minimum requirements to survive)

2. What others have (security, belonging, conforming)

3. What other people don't have (status)

With the aid of the social technology of money members of society organize to satisfy these three levels of desires. Ultimately the "system" a society employs determines how well desires are met, and how much energy concentrates and for what purposes. The "system", the social construct, matters a great deal. How much faith people place in the system; how fair and equal people perceive it to be; motivates people to make or take money. If too many people decide to take money the system corrodes and ultimately collapses.

Satisfying wants and needs, person by person, does not generate nearly as much energy as successfully employing a lever. The more wants and needs a person satisfies the more trust that person earns and the more energy he or she controls. The more desires a person satisfies, the more money he or she makes.

Systems in the developed world are so advanced, subsistence needs, for the most part, are met. Since men and women do not have to spend much time, energy and talent focusing on feeding and clothing themselves they focus instead on social desires: belonging and status. Most people in America are concerned about keeping up with the Jones's; on getting what other people have. A substantial, but smaller group of Americans are consumed with getting ahead; on getting what other people don't have. Maintaining social and economic parity is considered a "must have"; it's practically considered a "right" in America. Not achieving and sustaining a certain lifestyle makes one a failure; for many the greatest calamity of all.

Status commands a premium in America. Status is so important; the developed world has evolved a "cult of celebrity". Human beings are by nature king-makers. We build up select individuals, those with certain admirable qualities, and convey to those people a high degree of power. With this power flows attention and opportunities to acquire money.

In a "cult of celebrity" common people live vicariously through superstar performers, actors, sports heroes, and luminary political and industrial leaders. These celebrities, whether deserving of respect and admiration or not, are looked at by the population as more beautiful, wiser, more talented and or more insightful than ordinary men and women. Because they are afforded a special status they automatically command social power. People with social power attract attention. A cult of celebrity is a self-reinforcing cycle of the masses directing attention toward celebrities. This attention conveys energy; potential power, to that celebrity.

Where people direct attention, energy follows. Energy flows toward people others idolize. That energy is a great source of leverage. By gaining and maintaining more attention an individual controls more energy and potentially greater leverage.

People commit attention to changing how they feel. We all focus on satisfying desires. Wherever we direct our focus, our attention, energy flows. Energy flows where attention goes. Every energy flow represents a money making opportunity. By satisfying desires money-makers gain control of energy. Money flows where attention goes.

## Panning for Gold

- Do the best you can with what you've got.

- Who you are matters most.

- Get your core beliefs right.

- Expand your vision, fuel desire and focus on making, not taking, money.

- Wealth concentrates in relatively few hands.

- Those who serve the most, who satisfy the most desires, make the most money.

146

- Becoming prosperous is not a matter of looks or talent or education; making lots of money is a factor of applying leverage.

- Thought, the means to access infinite *source,* is an individual's most powerful lever.

- Effectively focusing people toward a common goal significantly increases leverage.

- Building a business leverages both sides of the desire-satisfaction equation. A business gives employees an opportunity to contribute while satisfying customers' desires.

- A mature, complex society builds systems to meet subsistence needs on a grand scale. In mature societies attention focuses on social needs of conforming (getting what others have) and status (getting what others don't have).

- Wherever people direct attention is an opportunity for making money.

- Energy flows where attention goes.

- To make money gain and maintain people's attention. The more attention one garners the more money one can potentially make.

147

# CHAPTER 16

# DO SOMETHING

**Every notable person in history did something; they did it.**

## Be Something

In life we feel, we act, and then we feel again. Most of us make the process automatic. We define our core beliefs then settle into habits to get through the minutia of everyday life. We produce and we consume. We give and we get. If we are ambitious and imaginative, connected and courageous; if we are self-less and generous we produce more than we consume. We contribute to the energy flow and experience a multitude of opportunities to make money.

If things are not unfolding as you had hoped; if what you are experiencing is not to your liking, something has to change. That "something" is not out there. That "something" is not circumstances. That "something" is you. You must change who you are. When you change yourself your experiences change; your opportunities change. Someday is not the perfect time. The perfect time is now. First, be something, then do something. Then you can have anything.

An economy is a feeling–acting–feeling system. It's a process of energy conversion, energy transformation. Energy is constantly moving, constantly flowing from person to person. Money is made by contributing to that system.

People are always trying to change how they feel. To make money; help them. You can meet wants and needs; you can satisfy desires. If you are not naturally inclined to make money, if you can't seem to get in the flow, then you must first change course. You must break the pattern, the habits you have settled into. You must do, what is for many, the most difficult of all tasks: you must **think**, and by thinking connect with unlimited *source*.

Thinking is a human beings ultimate power. Thought is the bridge from the tangible material world to *infinite intelligence* and unlimited *source*. Thought is how the energy of ideas flow. Insight, wisdom and inspiration come from the *source*, from *infinite intelligence*.

## THE THOUGHT PROCESS

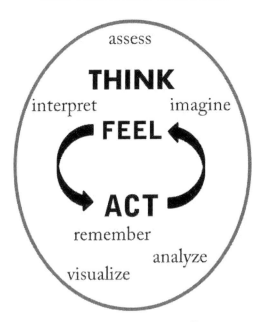

**Thought connects us to *Source***

Tune in to the *source*. Set yourself on a new course. Take control of the feeling–acting–feeling process. Life need not just happen to you. Life is meant to happen through you. Engage your mind. Change how you feel and change what you do. Empower yourself. Open the floodgates; draw energy from the *source* and channel that energy. You possess a lever large enough to move the world. The answers are not out there, they are inside you. Think.

Scarcity is not a natural state of the human condition. Our world, this reality is one of abundance. Challenges arise not because of the natural order, but because of the social order. How "things" are distributed, how needs are met, and where energy flows is a collective social decision. People make the world go round. People make the energy of an economy flow. And people disrupt that flow.

Someone who desires to make money, who intends to make money, has two options: 1) Go where the energy is flowing; or 2) Generate a new flow. Making money is fundamentally about creating and delivering value by contributing to the flow of energy. That energy satisfies every desire; and meets every want and need. There is always enough.

Seven billion, three-hundred million people inhabit this planet. Each one, every individual is a potential source of energy; a conduit fueling the economy. Every person has access to *infinite intelligence* and unlimited supply and can contribute to the flow of energy. All any person must do is choose to release the energy they encounter. When a person chooses to channel *source* energy into the world they create and contribute. Every opportunity to create and contribute is an opportunity for a person to do the best she can with what she's got. And that is always enough.

## It's All Right Here

This section is not designed to define in detail the mathematics of the energy of money. It is meant to give you a sense of an energy perspective. Play with the formulas. Work the ideas through in your mind. It will all become clear. If formulas and equations are not your thing, don't worry about the mathematical particulars. As long as you understand the fundamentals you can put yourself on the right track; in the flow of energy; the money-go-round.

Physics is the branch of science concerned with the nature and properties of matter and energy. Physics explores and defines how the energy of the physical world works. Physics tells us the energy of a system is the sum of the potential energy (PE) (inherent energy of a body or system not in motion) and the kinetic energy (KE) (energy in motion).

## Energy of System = PE + KE

Consider the energy of those **7.3 billion people (Energy of People: EoP)**; the energy of desires (to consume and produce) in process and yet to be expressed. Consider all the leverage contained in all the systems and products human beings have built over thousands of years; **the Residual Energy (or value) of Labor in every manmade thing (REoL)**. Then add in the **Energy of the Natural World (ENW)**.

## Energy of Economy = EoP + REoL + ENW

We can calculate the energy in our economy. If we work through the computation it would total a colossal sum. There is no shortage of energy. Making money is a matter of contributing to the energy flow; of making things happen. Opportunities are not limited and neither are you.

Feeling and thinking set the conditions for making money, but to see the process through requires **action**. Taking action, concentrating personal efforts toward some end, converts potential energy to kinetic energy and money changes hands. Making money is the process of converting potential energy to kinetic energy; the process of transforming energy by changing how people feel; by meeting wants and needs, satisfying desires.

The first law of thermodynamics states energy can neither be created nor destroyed, it just changes form. An economy is an energy system; an energy system driven by people's desires. Energy in an economy behaves in predictable ways. Money making opportunities can be expressed in energy equation terms. The challenge is converting physical energy units into social energy expressions. But that conversion has already been done. We express social energy units in money terms: dollars, Euros, Yen, Yuan and so on.

Here are a few energy equations to help express the nature of energy in a money system. We will convert the physical energy expressions to money expressions.

The potential energy (PE) of an object is that object's mass, multiplied by the force of gravity, multiplied by the height of the object:

## PE of an Object = mass x gravity x height

Force is a unit measure of energy.

Work is a unit measure of energy applied over a distance (calculating work considers resistance but for our purposes we will ignore resistance).

## Work = Force • Distance

Power is a unit measure of energy applied over a distance while also considering time. Power is expressed as work divided by the time it takes to complete that work:

## Power = Work / time

or

## Power = Force • Distance / time

Since money is energy we can consider money as a factor of force, distance and time (money is commonly associated with work). Substituting money for power; leverage for force; and desires fulfilled (number of desires) for distance, we get:

## Money = Leverage • # Desires / time

The potential energy of an economic opportunity (money) is a function of the force applied through leverage, multiplied by the number of desires satisfied, all divided by the time it takes to complete the process. These are the calculations business people make when they attempt to define the size of a market. Business people use different terms however, they use terms like demand and production and transportation costs and so on.

The challenge, or opportunity, when considering a business prospect is that desires can be unpredictable. Ultimately people are after feelings, how specifically they realize a new feeling varies. More important than the specific thing, product or service is the flow of energy.

John Stuart Mill, an 18th Century economist and philosopher refined a concept known as the "quantity theory of money". Economists employ the theory to determine how money flows through an economy. The equation also helps them forecast inflation and calculate the effects of monetary and fiscal policy. The equation can help us understand how an economy works.

$$M \cdot V = P \cdot Q$$

In this version of the equation of exchange "M" represents money, the medium of exchange. "V" is velocity; how quickly money moves from hand to hand, from person to person. "P" is a given price level of goods and services; the value people have settled on, what they are willing to pay for products and services; and Q represents outputs.

Restating the equation of exchange in more basic terms: the currency of trust, multiplied by people's intensity of desire (their willingness and urgency to change how they feel), equals the price people will pay, multiplied by the number of outputs or transactions. Money multiplied by velocity equals price multiplied by transactions. Said another way; trust in motion equals what people, in aggregate, value.

A recession or depression occurs when the velocity of trade slows down. This is when people either lose personal energy or confidence (desire and drive diminish), determine not to convert potential energy into kinetic energy (save money) or they lose faith in the system; in the currency of trust. When trust erodes people become reluctant to engage in trade and the economy slows down. As energy flow lessens an economy contracts. There is not less energy available in the system. Money is either being held as potential energy or trust has evaporated undermining the system.

Energy is neither created nor destroyed, it just changes form.

## Do Something

An economy is a social system. Money is a social technology; the currency of trust. The entire system is based on the premise of people serving people, of satisfying desires. To make money you must do something, you must create and contribute. You must help people get what they want. You must satisfy people's desires.

How much money anyone makes is a factor of how much energy he or she controls. To make money one must create and contribute value. That value contributes to the energy flow of an economy.

The way to increase the energy you control is by employing leverage. To make lots of money employ lots of leverage. Just understand, leverage works both ways; it can work against you as well as work for you. Be smart about employing leverage.

The money creation process is:

## Self > Assess Desires > Create > Contribute

First, get yourself straight. Get you core beliefs right. In order to make money align with truth: this is world of opportunity; you are connected and capable; and you have a purpose for being. Use the power of thought to connect with unlimited *source*. Determine a need. Figure out what desires people are looking to satisfy; what problems need to be solved. Create a solution to those problems; a way to satisfy those desires. Then deliver the value you create. Direct energy to connect with people in need. Help people get what they want and monetize your efforts.

To make more money, employ greater leverage.

The money that flows to you; the currency of trust; is energy you control. You can use that energy to create more value and amass more wealth. You can use that energy to consume or you can hold on to that energy as potential energy for future use. Amassing wealth is controlling the process of creation.

You have all you need. There is no such thing as scarcity; nothing is in short supply. There is more than enough energy to meet every material need of every human being on earth. We collectively however, have decided to concentrate wealth. Most people don't know how things work and are willing to settle for just getting by. A substantial segment of the population believes they must compete to survive and thrive. If they have trouble making money they resort to taking it. Then there is a small minority of people who make money; who create and contribute lasting value. These prosperous people make the money-go-round.

Through thought, your capacity of mind, you have access to *infinite intelligence* and unlimited supply; to the *source*. It is up to you whether you open the hatch and let *source* energy flow through you into this world.

The foundation of making money is the "self". Work on yourself. Making money, controlling the flow of energy is not an external reality, it is an internal capacity. Foster your ability to create and contribute; to generate and direct the flow of energy. Money is energy; a component of the energy of life. Your relationship to money, the abundance or lack which manifests in your experience is a reflection of how you are playing the game; how you are managing the energy of life.

To make money do things a certain way. Conform to the laws of life:

**1. Life intends to grow.**

**2. Thoughts become things.**

**3. Effort before reward.**

Grow as a person in knowledge, in compassion, in energy, in wisdom. Think, meditate, pray; connect with *source*. Humble yourself and become what you are meant to be; a conduit for the energy of life. Go with the flow. Find out where energy is flowing; what people want; what people are paying attention to. And give. Help people get what they want.

As you give of yourself and your endless supply of energy, you create a vacuum which fills automatically. When you give, you get; not always in the form of money; but when you create and contribute genuine value you always receive a reward. Be open to those rewards. Cherish what you have and what you get. There is nothing to be but grateful.

When it comes to making money realize it's a social endeavor. Because human beings are making the rules don't fixate on fairness. Life does not appear to be fair. Don't fixate on rights. You don't have a right to anything; you already have everything you need. Don't fixate on equality. Everyone is different, but everyone is of the same substance and from and connected to the same unlimited *source*. Get in the flow. Create and contribute. By creating and contributing you fuel the economy. And by creating and contributing you open yourself to opportunities to make money. You earn trust and trust makes all things possible.

People make what matters. People determine what matters. People value what matters. The energy of people is what matters most. Wherever people direct their attention energy follows. Energy flows where attention goes. To make money focus; focus on the right things. Focus on where the energy is flowing.

If your objective is to have money, focus on opening the flow. Focusing on creating value, helping people get what they want. The more potential energy you want to control the more leverage you need. Employ some leverage. But don't ever lose sight of the truth. Money is not about status or power. Money is not a thing to hoard or flaunt. Money is the currency of trust, the energy of an economy. If you choose to join the dance, then delight in the dance.

Every notable man and women in history joined the dance. They did something. They made things happen. They manipulated energy. They created and contributed to the energy flow. You can too. Make money. Do something!

## Panning for Gold

- Making money is a process of contributing to the energy flow.

- Change your habits; change your life.

- Thought is the ultimate asset. Thought connects people to infinite *source*.

- Typically people feel then act then feel again. Break the cycle and redirect energy by thinking.
- This is an abundant reality; there is no shortage of energy. We human beings however, have created a distribution gap.
- When it comes to making money, action is essential.
- The energy of an economic system behaves in accordance with natural law.
- Wishing, hoping, dreaming are all good places to start, but if you intend to make money, do something.
- Get your mindset straight; find a need to satisfy; create and contribute.
- To make more money, employ greater leverage.
- Follow the laws of life: life intends to grow; thoughts become things; and effort before reward. No one can break the law.
- You have everything you need. Go with the flow. Be a conduit for the energy of life.
- It's never "just business"; it's always about people.

# CHAPTER 17

# PROSPECTORS, MINERS AND MERCHANTS

# PANNING FOR GOLD

**You'd be wealthy if you converted your weight in gold into the currency of trust.**

## Strike it Rich

All of us are potential prospectors, miners and merchants. To make money we prospect for needs and wants to satisfy. We then mine the treasure we find, forging something to convert feelings of desire into feelings of satisfaction. As merchants we deliver our creation to fulfill those desires. The process of connecting with people and exchanging what we create monetizes our efforts. As prospectors, miners and merchants we keep the currency of trust flowing.

Not everyone has the desire or the constitution to be prospector, miner and merchant. Entrepreneurs and business builders are a rare breed. They prospect, make a find (a prospective want or need to satisfy; a market niche), and then figure out the details. They enlist the talent with the ideas and labor to create a system for satisfying wants and needs. Most people, rather than designing and building systems, choose to contribute to someone else's system. Most people, to get what they desire, trade their talents, expertise, energy and time for a wage. For those with an eye for treasure, an intellect and disposition for figuring it out, and the drive to act and see it through the prospect for making money is always exceptional.

Making money is a science. The process is as exacting as the "hard" sciences. Results are as definite as natural law. The challenge with making money is that even though one may comprehend the theory, actually applying the theory and manipulating energy is an art. A true artist masters basic skills and then advances the craft.

Here are the nuggets you have been searching for. Become a prospector, a miner and a merchant, then a true artist: master the basics then go on to create lasting value to your heart's content.

## One Big Process of Manipulating Energy

- **Money is a form of energy; a social compact; the currency of trust.** When held, money represents potential energy. When put to work money becomes kinetic energy.

- **Life is a feeling-action-feeling adventure.** Human beings experience a need or want, a desire to fulfill; then act to satisfy that desire; then feel again.

- **An economy is a dynamic *feeling conversion process*.** We use the economic process of production, distribution and delivery of goods and services to change how people feel.

- **Desire drives the economic system.**  Wants and needs, desires, cause people to act; to produce and consume. Desires drive trade and commerce.

- **People value most what people create and contribute.** What makes most things valuable are the ideas and action, the labor and energy people contribute.

- **Energy flows where attention goes.**  People pay attention to, focus on and devote time, energy and effort toward what they value.

- **Making money is the process of creating and contributing; of directing energy to convert feelings**. Creating is the process of adding value.  Value added is monetized when it is delivered to satisfy people's desires.

- **Gaining and maintaining people's attention is the surest way to make money.**  People pay attention to and will pay for what they value, so add value.

- **Thought is the means to control, guide and direct energy**.  Thought connects us with infinite *source*.  We receive, interpret and manipulate ideas through thought, then concentrate and direct energy through action.

- **The science of making money is the exact process of manipulating the flow of energy; the currency of trust.** The process consists of four steps:
1. Get yourself together; oriented in the right direction.
2. Identify a need or desire to satisfy or a problem to solve.
3. Create a means to satisfy the desire or solve the problem.
4. Deliver that creation; let the energy flow.


## Foreword:  Make It or Take It

- People can make money or take money.
- Making money is a creative, value-generating and life-enhancing process.
- Making money is being a conduit for energy to flow into and through the world.
- Taking money is a coercive, destructive and ultimately life-draining process.
- Taking money is siphoning off energy from an existing flow.
- The choice is always yours.  Choose to make it, not take it.

# Part 1

# Money Makes the World Go Round

- What we think of as "money" is really a social compact, a social technology facilitating the flow of energy: the exchange of ideas, goods and services.

- Money facilitates the functioning of our economic system; the process of people getting what they want; the process of satisfying desires.

- Money is always and only a means to a new feeling.

## Chapter 1: Family Money

- Focus on existing opportunities or create new opportunities.

- Acquire "valuable" knowledge.

- Build, nurture and sustain relationships with people you trust.

- Take calculated risks.

- Do what you say you will do, and deliver value.

## Chapter 2:  Money, Money, Money

- The traditional definition of money (medium of exchange, unit of account, store of value) does not go far enough.

- Money streamlines the process of trade, saving time, energy and effort.

- Money promotes the specialization of labor.

- As more people trusted in the medium, money became synonymous with the things money could buy.

- Not everything money offers is an advance.

- Money alters the political and social landscape.

- Money is impersonal.

- Money frees up political power and unshackles ambition and desire.

- A monetary system incorporates the element of time in a system of trading and tracking credits and debits.

- Money is a sophisticated social technology we employ to order our world.

## Chapter 3: The Currency of Trust

- People are the key component of the social system of money.

- Human beings establish value.

- Wants and needs, desires, determine value. Desire constitutes demand. To satisfy desires people create supply.

- Fundamentally an economic system is about relationships. However, a money system allows relationships to be less personal.

- The experience of life is all about feeling. Supply and demand; satisfying desires is a process of converting feelings.

- Money is a proxy for what people can have, do or become.

- Money is a social compact; an instrument of trust.

- After survival the most pervasive force in the human psyche is the drive for power. *Money, power, property* have evolved as a series of surrogates. Money is power.

- Money is useful only if it leads to happiness.

- Money is energy, the currency of trust.

## Chapter 4:  A Means to an End

- Money is a psychological store of value.  Money is intangible; most often it is a series of digits on account.

- Money is not the only way to enliven trust.  Personal relationships are still essential.

- Though money is not the only way, many people have determined money is the best way to get what they want.

- Since people can buy virtually anything, many people believe money can buy happiness, and therefore money is happiness.

- The system, an economic system, a system of money, only works to the degree people trust in it and in each other.  The real power of money, the currency of trust, resides in the energy of people.

- Money is always and only a means to an end.  That end is a new feeling.  Money is a means to help people feel.

- Since people put so much trust in money, money itself becomes the motive to act; the means to unleash creative human energy.

- Human beings are the economy. Money is a convenient artificial way to transfer trust. An economy still depends on people; people doing something.

- Making money is the process of generating energy; unleashing potential energy, adding value and helping people convert feelings: satisfy wants and needs.

- To amass wealth help other people get what they want. When you help others get what they want, those people will transfer trust to you.

- To master the science of making money learn what people want and how relationships work.

# Part 2
# Let's Get Down to Business

- People satisfying desires make the money go round.

- We are all in the people business; really the feelings business.

- To make lots of money employ leverage.

## Chapter 5: Empire Building

- Everything you get in life is a gift from God, share it.

- Do what needs to be done.

- Let money serve you rather than become a slave to money.

- Learn all you can.

- Earn trust by working hard and being exacting, tenacious and honest.

- Take control of your own destiny.

- Collaborate with trustworthy, capable people.

- Leverage money intelligently.

- Be willing to change direction if opportunities arise.

- Add value wherever you can.

- Conserve value and improve efficiencies where possible.

- Give as much as you can.

## Chapter 6: The Money-Go-Round

- The U.S. money supply is comprised of nearly $12 Trillion.

- Money represents "potential energy" when held and "kinetic energy" when employed.

- The U.S. economy produced about $17.4 Trillion worth of goods and services in 2014.

- Value is not fixed or static; it changes.

- People determine value.

- People ultimately value feelings. Any and every thing is only a means to convert feelings.

- Life is a feeling-action-feeling process.

- Wants and needs, desires, are virtually limitless.

- The processes of production, distribution and consumption; what makes markets and economies; are all a means to convert feelings.

- Value, as measured by money, is a function of satisfying wants and needs: fulfilling desires; converting feelings.

- Making money is creating value to convert feelings.

- Supply and demand are set by a sense of lack. This sense of lack is motivation to act.

- Human beings are the economy. People make the money go round.

- Understanding and serving people, fulfilling desires, is the way to prosperity.

## Chapter 7: Time Travels & Power Surges

- We are all in the people business; really the feelings business.

- Businesses make money by helping people get what they want; by changing how they feel.

- Human beings value most what human beings do.

- Collaborating to create value offers definite and distinct advantages.

- Time is our most precious asset.

- The residual value of labor; the ideas and action people contribute; endure in what those people make.

- Any thing containing the enduring value of labor offers leverage.

- Where energy surges opportunities abound.

- Money is made by generating, manipulating and directing surging energy.

## Chapter 8:  Pull the Levers

- Eighty percent of results stem from twenty percent of efforts.  We are surrounded by the "vital few" and the "trivial many".

- Equality only exists in theory.  Energy is always flowing; concentrating and scattering.

- People automatically and naturally stratify.

- People ascribe power to certain characteristics, traits and social factors.  These can be leveraged.

- Societies, like individuals, stratify.  Social power always concentrates in the hands of a few.

- A lever or pulley is a device offering a mechanical advantage.  To make money find and employ points of leverage.

- Leverage is usually a product of people.  Employing leverage is the process of using other people's energy, ideas, and money.

# Part 3

# The People Business

- Your core beliefs, your powerful, personal beliefs, will either propel you forward or hold you back.
- All money-making opportunities come by way of other people, no exceptions.
- Energy ebbs and flow; go to with the flow.

## Chapter 9:  Empowering Everyone

- It's good to be born with advantages, but everyone has advantages; success is a matter of developing and exploiting those advantages.

- Vision, drive and the willingness to take risks are distinguishing traits of achievers.

- Competition is most helpful when it improves performance.

- Find partners you respect and trust.

- There is no time like the present to get started.

- Go with the tide; ride the wave.

- Dream big dreams, and then turn those dreams into reality.

- Take calculated risks.

- Build a team, a high-performance team to achieve outstanding results.

- Leverage relationships to exploit opportunities and create value.

- Go for it.

## Chapter 10: How Life Works

- Life operates by certain laws; rules of the game. To make money comply with these rules:

  o Life Intends to Grow.

  o Thoughts Become Things.

  o Effort before Reward.

- Core beliefs are the lens through which people see the world. Core beliefs influence everything a person does.

- Core beliefs are the powerful, personal beliefs a person holds about the nature of this world, his or her capabilities and connections, and his or her purpose for being.

- Two personal forces propel or inhibit people's advance: drive and fear. These forces, though common to everyone, are not equally powerful in everyone.

- Any individual can boost his or her drive and overcome fear.

- Human beings have a built-in energy conservation device known as the "*habits process*".

- Habits are routine actions executed to satisfy specific desires. Habits take thought out of the equation.

- Typically people feel, then act, then feel. Life is a feeling-action-feeling process.

- We can use our *habits process* to change beliefs. By changing what we do, results change. With new results, beliefs begin to change.

- Change habits, change lives.

## Chapter 11: Can't Go it Alone

- A monetary system is meant to help people.

- The power in an economy is the social currency of trust. The greater the number of people involved in an economy, the more opportunity and potentially the more power.

- Making money is purely and always a social endeavor. There is no going it alone.

- The intermediary of money, allows people to treat business as impersonal.

- Working together people are more capable and powerful than they are working separately.

- The dominant economic worldview is one of scarcity.

- Scarcity is always and only a social construct.

- Believing in scarcity causes "unproductive" competition.

- All opportunities to make money come by way of other people, no exceptions.

- Every individual must decide to compete or collaborate.

- Consumption and production are social components of a social system. People represent both sides of the economic equation: supply and demand.

- To make money, cultivate relationships with people to serve, and people who produce.

- Success making money is a factor of success cultivating productive relationships.

# Chapter 12:  Something Bigger than Me

- Politicians and central bankers cannot control human behavior.

- The "business cycle" is a social cycle representing the energy flow in economic activity.

- The business cycle has four phases: expansion, boom, contraction, and bust.

- Cycles are an aspect of the natural and social world.

- Energy ebbs and flows through human generations.

- A generational cycle lasts approximately eighty years.

- A generational cycle moves through four phases: a high (pulling together), an awakening (drifting apart), an unraveling (division and conflict) and a crisis era (creative destruction leading to the renewal of a high).

- Each generation has a role to play in these social cycles.

- We are now in the midst of the winter season, the crisis era.

- Cycles and seasons are bigger than individuals.

- The best anyone can do is recognize the cycle and prepare accordingly.

- Making money, creating value, is about pulling together. We are in the crisis era, the time of greatest risk, and greatest opportunity.  It is time to pull together.

# Part 4

# Alchemy

# All that Glitters Isn't Gold

- Make money by doing things a certain way.
- Money flows where attention goes.
- You have everything you need.  Do something; open the floodgates and let the energy flow.

## Chapter 13:  That's Entertainment

- Focus on your strengths; what you love to do and do best.
- Keep embracing new opportunities.
- Share your talent, your joy, your love.
- Help people genuinely feel.
- Put your heart into what you do.
- Keep going, despite challenges; never give up.
- Get people's attention and go with the flow.

- People have nothing but time and opportunity to feel.
- People's attention is drawn to flowing energy.
- People naturally idolize men and women who help them feel.
- Where attention goes, money flows.

## Chapter 14: Something from Nothing

- Making money is the process of transforming something ordinary into something extraordinary.
- Life is not all about the money. Life is about feeling, experiencing, and being.
- Not everything can be monetized.
- Economic exchange is a process of energy conversion.
- Economic benefit is derived from ideas and action.
- Doing things a certain way produces a certain result.
- Wants and needs energize the economic system.
- Money changes from potential energy to kinetic energy as it moves from person to person; as feelings change.
- Trillions of dollars are on the move around the world.
- All people are producers and consumers.
- People who amass wealth consistently produce more than they consume.
- Anyone can make money by doing things a certain way.

- Money represents energy, potential energy. Having money means having control of potential energy.

- Scientific Money Making Process: Self > Identify Need > Create > Deliver

- Making money is one way of contributing to life's energy flow.

## Chapter 15: Energy Flows Where Attention Goes

- Do the best you can with what you've got.

- Who you are matters most.

- Get your core beliefs right.

- Expand your vision, fuel desire and focus on making, not taking, money.

- Wealth concentrates in relatively few hands.

- Those who serve the most, who satisfy the most desires, make the most money.

- Becoming wealthy is not a matter of looks or talent or education; making lots of money is a factor of applying leverage.

- Thought, the means to access infinite *source*, is an individual's most powerful lever.

- Effectively focusing people toward a common goal significantly increases leverage.

- Building a business leverages both sides of the desire satisfaction equation. A business gives its employees an opportunity to contribute while satisfying customers' desires.

- A mature, complex society builds systems to meet subsistence needs on a grand scale. In mature societies attention focuses on social needs of conforming (getting what others have) and status (getting what others don't have).

- Wherever people direct attention is an opportunity for making money.

- Energy flows where attention goes.

- To make money gain and maintain people's attention. The more attention one garners the more money one can potentially make.

## Chapter 16: Do Something

- Making money is a process of contributing to the energy flow.

- Change your habits; change your life.

- Thought is the ultimate asset. Thought connects people with infinite *source*.

- Typically people feel then act then feel again. Break the cycle and redirect energy by thinking.

- This is an abundant reality; there is no shortage of energy. We human beings however, have created a distribution gap.

- When it comes to making money, action is essential.

- The energy of an economic system behaves in accordance with natural law.

- Wishing, hoping, dreaming are all good places to start, but if you intend to make money, do something.

- Get your mindset straight; find a need to satisfy; create and contribute.

- To make more money, employ greater leverage.

- Follow the laws of life: life intends to grow; thoughts become things; and effort before reward. No one can break the law.

- You have everything you need. Go with the flow. Be a conduit for the energy of life.

- It's never "just business"; it's always about people.

# AFTERWORD

We all want to be wealthy. We all want to revel in abundance and prosperity. While we are at it lets state the whole truth: we want to be good looking and popular; and we want to be lean and fit and strong and athletic; we want to be smart and witty and quick and funny; and we want to be talented and capable; and visionary and innovative and creative. Seems like a pretty tall order. We want to have more, do more and be more. We want it all.

Can we have it all?

Why not? Why not have it all, do it all and be it all?

We human beings are a curious lot. We have countless gifts and talents; unlimited assets and resources; and access to power beyond comprehension, but we sometimes, too often, focus on the most inane activities and engage in the most trivial, but not inconsequential of games. Instead of making the most of opportunities; instead of conquering fear; instead of letting go of what holds us back; instead of soaring to great heights we struggle, we settle and then we blame. We stumble at the starting gate and then instead of pressing forward wallow in self-pity. We think we don't know what to do or which way to go.

Too many spend their lives wandering lost when the truth, about money, about health, about relationships, about life, is flashing like a neon sign before them. Don't be one of the lost souls; don't choose to be a victim.

This adventure called life consists of two elements: time and opportunity. To have it all, make the most of what you have; make the most of time and opportunity.

So far in life you have been doing things in just the right way to get what you've got. Sometimes you may have prospered, and sometimes you may have fallen short. But you always, without fail, with scientific rigor and regularity, achieved the results you set into motion. The outcome you produced, the circumstances you manifested were the exact, repeatable and verifiable result of the formula you implemented.

If you have not yet built the wealth you aspire to, you have not yet implemented the right formula. You've not yet applied the right science.

You have before you, like you always have had, the opportunity to choose. You may have always thought money, wealth, abundance and prosperity were for the select, perhaps lucky few. And you may have determined you just aren't lucky. Luck has nothing to do with it.

There is a science to making money. There is a science to becoming wealthy. You don't have to become a scientist; you just have to do things a certain way to get the results you desire. Science is about determining and applying absolutes; the laws of nature, the laws of life.

The distance from where you are now to where you desire to be is not far. Seeing with new vision, hearing with new clarity and acting with new purpose is a choice. You have the ability to create. What do you want to create?

Do not procrastinate. Do not rationalize and make excuses. Do not judge and condemn and place blame. It is people's tendency to do these things that holds them back. Try something new, something different instead and consider what if...

Instead of procrastinating embrace opportunity. Instead of judging, condemning and blaming, yourself and others, accept what is and set about creating something better. And instead of rationalizing and making excuses just move forward.

Follow the process, the money making process. Follow the steps and you will produce the results. Advance despite fear. Create and contribute. You can have more, do more and be more. Just apply the science.

One more thing. Feedback is essential for making course adjustments and improving performance. Getting your feedback regarding *Money, The New Science of Making It* will help me refine key points as I present this material. Please email your thoughts to:

Scott@c-achieve.com

Thank you.

*Scott F. Paradis*

# ACKNOWLEDGEMENTS

Everything I have done, everything I do, and everything I am yet to accomplish is made possible by the loving and supportive people who surround me and by those that are drawn into my awareness. My success is made possible by God's inspiration and the genius and generosity of countless people.

For Lisa, my wife, and my two terrific children, Merideth and Mitchell, and all my family and friends I am forever grateful. I am truly blessed having wonderful people in my life.

To past sages, modern day prophets, and those searching diligently to express truth through insightful words and faithful examples I extend my most heartfelt thanks. The courage, commitment and sacrifice of men and women who embrace the opportunity that is life inspire me. I pray that the words etched on these pages might inspire you to take on laudable challenges, endure worthwhile hardships, and fulfill what I know to be limitless potential.

# ABOUT THE AUTHOR

Scott F. Paradis is a student of life and a seeker of ultimate truth. His current focus is on health and wealth. Striving to simplify the complex he studies human performance and potential through the disciplines of economics, business, human relations, communications, politics, philosophy, religion, athletics, and health and fitness. He intends to discern simple, enduring truths; the wisdom of life. Only once something is made simple can we, do we, truly understand.

A native of New Hampshire, as of this writing Scott lives in northern Virginia where he concluded a 30-year career with the United States Army. He is married to a shining star, the former Lisa Newcombe, and has two extraordinary adult children: Merideth and Mitchell.

Attempting to lead by example Scott helps people live full and fulfilling lives. He helps people dream big and build faith by establishing life-affirming habits of thinking, feeling and acting. And he helps people relate to others and life in positive, fulfilling ways.

Scott retired from the Army at the rank of colonel. In addition to varied stateside assignments he completed tours in Europe and the Middle East. He served as a National Security Fellow with the John F. Kennedy School of Government at Harvard University and as a National Defense Congressional Fellow with the United States Senate. He holds a Master of Science in Administration from Central

Michigan University and a Bachelor of Arts in Sociology from the University of New Hampshire.

Scott's personal aspiration is for his life to be a message of hope, an example of faith, and an expression of love as he works to do the best he can with what he's got.

# *Success101Workshop.com*

# *(703) 772-3521*

***Success 101 Workshop*** is all about improving **performance** and helping people **live life to the fullest**. Through inspiring presentations and engaging workshops, focused on fundamentals, we strive to simplify the seemingly complex.

To learn a task, to improve, to master something, focus on the fundamentals. Once you master the fundamentals there's no stopping you.

*Through consultations, presentations and workshops, online courses and books **Success 101 Workshop*** shows individuals how to have more, do more and become more. We throw open the curtains obscuring simple truths. We help people see the big picture and imagine exciting new possibilities. Then we help them get moving in the right direction.

Success, in business and in life, is not a matter of commanding irresistible power and employing overwhelming resources, it is a matter of doing the best you can with what you've got. You have more assets at your disposal than you know. By relying on your natural abilities and learning and leveraging the fundamental principles of success you can change your body, your mind, your business: your life. Yes you really can.

You have potential you haven't yet begun to tap. Contact us now, we can help.

**Available from***:*
*Scott F. Paradis*
*Success101Workshop*
*Success101Workshop.com*
*&*
*Cornerstone Achievements*

**Books:**

*Money*
*The New Science of Making It*

*High Performance Habits Health and Fitness Habits*
*Engage Your Health and Fitness Auto-Pilot*

*High Performance Habits*
*Making Success a Habit*

*How to Succeed at Anything*
*In 3 Simple Steps*

*Success 101 How Life Works*
*Know the Rules, Play to Win*

*Promise and Potential*
*A Life of Wisdom, Courage, Strength and Will*

*Warriors Diplomats Heroes, Why America's Army Succeeds*
*Lessons for Business and Life*

**Look for these online courses offered by Scott F. Paradis:**

*Money, The New Science of Making It*

*High Performance Health and Fitness Habits,*
*Engage your Health and Fitness Auto-Pilot*

*High Performance Habits, Making Success a Habit*

*Success 101 How to Succeed, Focus on Fundamentals*

*Success 101 How Life Works, Know the Rules, Play to Win*

*High Performance Leadership,*
*Fundamental Leadership Habits*

*Loving 101, Making Love a Habit*

*Be, A Messenger of Hope, an Example of Faith and an*
*Expression of Love*

**Contact us to schedule a presentation, a consultation or a performance oriented workshop (703) 772-3521.**

44686312R00115

Made in the USA
Charleston, SC
31 July 2015